SIMPLE
PLEASURES

PL△INSPOKEN
Real-life stories of
Amish and Mennonites

"Woven with insights, humor, and deeply-seated spiritual wisdom, mother and wife Marianne Jantzi opens her home and heart as she recounts her real-life experiences, offering fresh and honest perceptions of the Amish."
—*Kate Lloyd, author of* The Legacy of Lancaster Trilogy (CBA *bestsellers* Leaving Lancaster, Pennsylvania Patchwork, *and* Forever Amish*)*

"This charming story of a mother and her family will have the reader alternately chuckling, reminiscing, and pondering with pleasure the small everyday events that make up the fullness of life in this Amish home. Jantzi is a natural storyteller, and her book is simply fun to read."
—*Karen M. Johnson-Weiner, professor of anthropology, author of* Train Up a Child: Old Order Amish and Mennonite Schools *and* New York Amish, *and coauthor of* The Amish *with Donald B. Kraybill and Steve Nolt*

"*Simple Pleasures* reminds me of a patchwork quilt. Each simple piece is stitched together with faith, family, and friendships, creating a beautiful whole. Jantzi offers a gentle reminder to savor the seemingly insignificant moments in time, for they fill us with love, warmth, and a feeling of well-being, just like a quilt."

—*Linda Maendel, author of* Hutterite Diaries: Wisdom from My Prairie Community

SIMPLE PLEASURES

Stories from My Life as an Amish Mother

MARIANNE JANTZI

Herald Press

Harrisonburg, Virginia
Kitchener, Ontario

Library and Archives Canada
Cataloguing in Publication

Jantzi, Marianne, author
    Simple pleasures : stories from my life as an Amish mother / Marianne Jantzi.

(Plainspoken: real-life stories of Amish and Mennonites)
ISBN 978-1-5138-0027-1 (paperback)
    1. Jantzi, Marianne. 2. Amish women—Canada—Biography. 3. Amish
women—Family relationships—Canada. 4. Mothers—Canada—Biography.
I. Title.
BX8129.A5J35 2016   305.48'68973   C2015-908662-0

Scriptures from *The Holy Bible, King James Version*.
"Is It Raining Little Flower?"; p. 46, from the collection *Honey from the Hive*,
collected by Joseph Stoll. Author unknown. Used by permission of Pathway
Publishers, Ontario.
"Ten O'clock Regrets," p. 100-101, first printed in *Family Life* magazine. Used by
permission of Pathway Publishers, Ontario.

SIMPLE PLEASURES
© 2016 by Herald Press, Kitchener, Ontario N2G 3R1
    Released simultaneously in the United States by Herald Press,
    Harrisonburg, Virginia 22802. All rights reserved.
Library of Congress Control Number: 2015960025
Canadian Entry Number: C2015-908662-0
International Standard Book Number: 978-1-5138-0027-1
Printed in United States of America
Cover and interior design by Merrill Miller
Cover photo by Bill Coleman, © NoToCo, LLC / AmishPhoto.com

Parts of most chapters in this book appeared previously in *The Connection*, a
monthly periodical that connects Amish communities, and are used with permission. For subscription information, call 1-888-333-2119.

For orders or information, call 1-800-245-7894 or visit HeraldPress.com.

20 19 18 17 16   10 9 8 7 6 5 4 3 2 1

*To my husband, Allan, who will never understand
itchy pens but tolerates them quite well;
and to my four children, Alyssa, Eric, Kyle, and Chloe,
who provide so many stories.*

CONTENTS

INTRODUCTION TO

P L △ I N S P O K E N

Real-life stories of Amish and Mennonites

AMISH NOVELS, Amish tourist sites, and television shows offer second- or third-hand accounts of Amish, Mennonite, and Hutterite life. Some of these messages are sensitive and accurate. Some are not. Many are flat-out wrong.

Now readers can listen directly to the voices of these Anabaptists themselves through Plainspoken. In the books in this series, readers get to hear Amish, Mennonite, and Hutterite writers talk about the texture of their daily lives: how they spend their time, what they value, what makes them laugh, and how they summon strength from their Christian faith and community.

Plain Anabaptists are publishing their writing more than ever before. But this literature is read mostly by other Amish, Mennonites, and Hutterites, and rarely by the larger public.

Through Plainspoken, readers outside their communities can learn what authentic plain Anabaptist life looks and feels like—from the inside out. The Amish and Mennonites and Hutterites have stories to tell. Through Plainspoken, readers get the chance to hear them.

Author's Note

TODAY I WASN'T SURE what I wanted to do after I had swept the kitchen floor.

But I never had a chance to choose. It was almost half past three when I swept the dirt onto the dustpan and tossed it in the trash can. I knew that after half past three, time takes care of itself. My oldest daughter, Alyssa, comes home from school, looking for a snack. Allan comes from his work, wanting supper. On its heels come cleanup, stories, baths, and bedtime.

Once again it feels as though the day is over before it begins. Though sometimes challenging, these are good days, filled with children, chores, customers, and laughs. Come join us.

In these pages you will meet my family, at various ages and stages of their life. Since this is a collection of journal writings, arranged by major topics, the size of our family and our ages change throughout the book.

Here they all are: By my side is my husband, Allan, whom I married July 26, 2006. We've been blessed beyond measure with Alyssa, January 18, 2008; Eric, December 8, 2009; Kyle, November 16, 2011; and Chloe, April 16, 2015.

It is my greatest wish that you leave these pages feeling encouraged.

• • •

A few additional explanations may help you follow my family's stories:

Doddy and Mommy Over There: Allan's parents live on the other end of our double house. Their house is easily accessible from a door in our kitchen, straight to their kitchen full of good food, candy, and listening ears. Uncle David lives with them. He enjoys jigsaw puzzles and playing dominoes.

Doddy and Mommy Far Away: My parents live a mile and a half up the road. My sister and brother—Aunt Kathryn and Uncle Jody—live there with them.

Susan and Laura: My married sisters who both live nearby.

The Connection: A periodical where I am a monthly columnist; my column is called Northern Reflections. It is widely distributed among the Amish groups of North America.

Circle letters: Written by groups of friends and relatives who communicate via letter. Each person adds a letter to the envelope before passing the pack on.

• • •

I will be forever grateful to Melodie Davis, managing editor at Herald Press, for patiently guiding me through the process of publishing a book. A special thanks to Amy Gingerich, editorial director, for visiting our home and for patiently answering my questions. Thank you, too, Dorothy Hartman, for providing organization and typing, and Craig Anderson in the Ontario office of MennoMedia for being a courier and scanner of the manuscript as it progressed.

Above all, thank you to my husband and children for allowing me to tell our stories.

—*Marianne Jantzi*

PART I

Little House Beside the Big House

1

The Dawdy Haus

HOME TO US is somewhere in the middle of the only original Old Order Amish settlement in Canada. The cozy little *Dawdy Haus* here at Allan's parents' place has suited our needs fine since our marriage in 2006. It only got cozier in January of 2008 when we squeezed in some baby furniture and little Alyssa arrived. As a toddler, she was tinier than most her age and kept us busy with the chattering, walking, running, and exploring end of things. My uncle declared then that she stole her mother's voice, but so far no one has commended me for losing mine.

• • •

My Allan is a lunch-bucket guy working in construction, like so many others around here. So far, so good with new jobs coming in. A couple of years ago we chose the most dilapidated of the numerous outbuildings here on Doddy's little four-acre lot and put up a tall new black-and-white shop. Then, lest his schoolteacher wife should miss her challenges too much, Allan framed part of it in for a boot and shoe store. Now I could face the test of starting my own business and keep figuring and working with students by helping them find quality footwear at fair prices. Of course, all easier said than done, but we do have a thriving business with huge potential for growth.

Maybe shoes aren't the best business for me. Back when I started teaching, my grade-one girls watched with wide eyes as I laced up my midcalf hiking shoes. Finally, one ventured bravely, "Miss Albrecht, are those yours?"

"Sure," I replied with a smile.

"Well, Miss Albrecht," she gasped, "they do not look like a mama's shoes!"

I wasn't even a mama at the time. Hopefully my tastes have changed?

The rest of that shop space isn't sitting idle. That's where we do our evening, weekend, and rainy day work. My dad's metal shop and time was filled, so he moved three punch presses in so we could make hangers for eaves troughs. Now, this job never has gotten exciting or challenging, but it's an easy, sit-down, no-brain job, plus good quality time with your better half. Of course the paycheck at the end gives ample motivation. For the mechanically minded, we run these presses without electricity using a diesel motor and hydraulics. Or does the diesel run the hydraulics? I just keep my nose and fingers out of that stuff.

So now you have a little taste of who we are. Let's look at the big picture—our community. How did we actually end up here in Canada being called Milverton Amish instead of in Lancaster, Pennsylvania; Holmes County, Ohio; or in Indiana somewhere? And why is it that this settlement only has eight districts and isn't even close to rivaling the originals in the United States?

It started in the 1700s with poor, penniless Christian Naffziger of Germany, who decided peasant farming was not getting him and his descendants anywhere. With the help of friends he moved safely to the community in Lancaster, Pennsylvania. But his poverty followed him, and already the land was out of his price range. However, he was encouraged to hear of free land in Canada. He felt confident that the Amish would be up to the challenge of clearing a two-rod strip of land along the front of a two-hundred-acre plot, building a cabin, and paying a small surveyor's fee, all for fifty free acres. According to often-told Amish stories, he dropped in to see the king in London, England just to be sure the offer was legitimate. King George or an associate assured him the deed was real and pressed a few gold coins into Christian's hand during the farewell handshake!

Christian's friends from Europe and Pennsylvania were encouraged by his reports, and many made the long, difficult trip to Canada. Here they received help from the nearby Waterloo Mennonite congregation. During the 1800s this church grew rapidly. There were numerous church splits, with one of the main reasons being the building of church houses. In our area, one deacon, two ministers, and some members refused church houses and continued to meet in one another's homes. From these few faithful members grew what is called the Old Order church today.

The other congregations are still around and are called Beachy Amish, New Order Amish, or Amish Mennonite, as well as other more-specific names. So here my family and community is today, probably because a poor man wanted better for his descendants.

2

A Queen Dethroned

"**N**OW YOU HAVE a million-dollar family," the kind old doctor announced to my husband. These words had nothing to do with winning a lottery but came after the birth of our son, Eric David. He arrived safe and sound on December 8, 2009, weighing six pounds eight ounces and measuring eighteen and a half inches long.

Big sister Alyssa was pleased or disgruntled, depending on the occasion, mood, or time of day. Our little man was born light haired and fair skinned, a trait he shares with his mom, whereas his older sister shares a dark complexion, hair, and eyes with her dad. Both are tiny and fine featured to match both parents, I guess.

Alyssa made sure that I held "her" baby. Thus the aunts, so kindly lending a hand with the work, and her daddy were "baby deprived." At times Alyssa would decide it was *her* turn for a cuddle from me, and then the others got their chance with the baby.

And we truly were a million-dollar family. I thanked God for two healthy children, loving and helpful extended family and friends, food, clothes, shelter, church, work, and the health and strength to enjoy these blessings.

• • •

When Alyssa was a baby I kept a white plastic basket stocked with soft clothes, a baby brush for her dark hair, good-smelling baby bath soap, shampoo, and lotion. When bath time came, I'd retrieve my basket and the fun would begin. The procedure always ended with a good rubdown with smooth, pink Johnson's baby lotion. Then I'd wrap her all cozy and warm in a fuzzy pink blanket and inhale her sweet baby scent.

When Eric arrived, I happily resumed the bath-time ritual, but no amount of bathing and lotion helped the raw, red rash under his neck and in his fat creases. Nor did it help his dry, scaly head, which was quickly losing its wispy brown hair. Finally, at the urging of Mom and Aunt Sarah we made a long-overdue trip to the doctor. I was surprised to find out that I was dealing with eczema.

The contents of the white plastic basket soon changed, and the bath-time ritual did too. Creamy white lotion, smelling like a sterile hospital room, was rubbed on the dry patches. Thick pasty diaper rash cream dried up the gooey spots. The baby brush disappeared just like Eric's hair.

Then I wrapped my baby all warm and cozy in a cotton blanket and breathed in the sterile hospital smell. It sure beat the foul smell of oozing eczema. There are ways to treat eczema symptoms, but no quick cure.

3

Frigid Days

WINTER IS OFTEN LOVELY HERE, though cold. Some days the winds are no more than stiff breezes and the sun shines often. A perfect "still" cold turns into an opportunity for smooth ice rinks at most of our eight private Amish schools. Two community rinks are also prepared. It reminds me of when the river froze over and the daddy here couldn't resist taking Alyssa, then two years old, to try her tiny skates.

"Like this, Mom!" she would demonstrate. "Whoosh, whoosh, whoosh," she said, gliding gracefully across the hardwood floor in her stocking feet. Daddy would raise his brows and give a look that said there would still be a few years until there was whoosh, whoosh gliding.

But most northern winters don't pass without a storm. One day in January, that is just what happened. The snow began to fall, the wind picked up and whipped around the snow that was already here, and the temperature dipped. We were all at home, cozy in our little house or working in our warm shop, when the news arrived. My friend Marianna, from Michigan, was on her way! I ran around in little circles and jabbered excitedly, wondering if she'd make it in the storm and what should I cook for her? Would I have time to bake something or what time did Allan suppose she'd be here?

I soon came to my senses and knew what I must do. Quickly, I washed the dishes and set them in the drain tray. Next I took the broom and tackled the floor. Then there she was—the same Marianna, running through the storm with their "little" boy, who had grown so much. Whew, she made it! She said she would never have started out if she had known about the whiteouts they would drive through. "You couldn't see ahead of you, but we kept going, not knowing what was coming behind. It was just terrible. I never drove in anything like it," she explained. I enjoyed her visit immensely, and thankfully she had a much better ride home the next day.

In the middle of the winter we still ride in an open buggy. We just huddle behind our big black umbrellas! But don't let this account of bad weather drive you away. By April the soft spring breezes are blowing with the promise of spring.

• • •

I read a detailed account of the Haitian earthquake back in 2010 written by a missionary mother. She vividly described the horrors of cries for help from under the rubble, work at the makeshift clinics, dump truck loads of bodies, the awful smell . . . and then she added her woes. She complained that she was growing weary of her bawling children. How dare she! Right there in the midst of mothers with hurt children, mothers who lost their children, and children who lost their mothers, she was complaining that her children were bawling! Oops, I'll stop short there. Wasn't it just last week that my house was too small, that it was such a long time since I last got groceries and my

children were . . . and to think that there are mothers in Haiti
. . . Lord, help me to stop this complaining and nitpicking.

Sometimes I even forget to be thankful for the door. I vowed
I would never, ever forget to be thankful for our door, and here's
why: For a long time there was only one way to properly enter
our little home, through a very ancient door. It was so ancient
that there were two doors. The first was a screen door with a
glass you put in for winter. Next you entered the storm door,
with its banana shape and wobbly knob. During the winter,
every time someone would exit that door, I would wipe my
hands on my apron and take a good hold of the knob while
pressing firmly at the bottom with my foot. With a bit of luck
the door would latch with the first try. Of course, the wind still
blew through its many cracks. If everyone was leaving home
for a long period, we'd first check the door, then exit through
Doddys' house to avoid the difficult closure. When the nice
weather came we didn't worry about the storm door. It just
hung open, waiting for rainy days to be put to use. As for the
screen door, there was a hole in the screen for the flies and it
had the most annoying screech every time you passed through!
I'd be working in the garden when I heard that screech and I'd
know Allan was home from work or one of my sisters had come
or there was an intruder around.

The new door does not have its own special alarm system,
but it is solid with a tight latch, and the winter gusts are kept
at bay. It has a wonderful, clear window with dividing frames
between the panes that make it a breeze to wash. Sometimes I
forget to be thankful for it, but not as often as I would if I hadn't
put up with the ancient one. I guess there's a reason we don't
always get what we want *right now*.

• • •

It's cold and snowy and blowy and I'm piling wood into the Pioneer Maid (our woodstove) and the shop furnace. Sewing, cleaning, cooking, and baking. I'm one of those homemakers who sends her man off to work each morning, then spends one day after the next cooped up inside with the little ones. Before you know it, you feel dull and listless and oversugared from eating and eating the cookies you made for the lunch box. So I invented my own little day brightener: every day the children and I go outside.

That was easy to say. Now we just have to do it.

First, I always think about how much time it's going to take and then look at my sewing, the dirty dishes, and the empty cookie jar. Then I take a deep breath and bundle children in thick coats, caps, scarves, boots, and mittens. Here we go in our trusty black ice-fishing sled that never did go ice fishing. We walk and play in the fresh, exhilarating air. Last winter, if we lasted fifteen minutes we were doing well. But the effects are long lasting. We all feel bright and refreshed and go at our work and play with more vigor. Maybe it even cuts down on our colds and cranky spells. At least it gives us something to talk about when Daddy comes home.

Back in my teaching days, the senior teachers used to drill and drill us to send our students outside to play. If they couldn't go outside, we were to give them exercise indoors. Get their hearts pumping and their blood flowing! Refresh those brains! And the teacher needs the refresher just as much as—or more than—the students do. I think this advice works well for mothers and preschoolers too.

I resolved to have a go-outside schedule to further ensure that I don't skip the dreary, rainy, or too-cold days. The secret is motivation and proper clothing. During the winters that we have had a new baby, I even take the baby outside on nice days, bundled into an infant car seat. (We use the car seat primarily when hiring a driver for car trips.)

I read an article by a fitness instructor that said we live in an age where we search for that miracle pill to cure our ills. He said we have to try harder to do this instead: (1) get enough sleep; (2) eat healthy and properly; (3) drink enough water; (4) get thirty minutes of exercise daily; (5) spend time alone to pray and meditate every day. These steps should eliminate some doctor visits and pills.

Of course there are always the challenges. The year Alyssa was born, it was cold and stormy. She joined us on January 18. That year I contentedly sat on the couch and watched the snow blow while I cared for my little pink bundle. We had a good winter even without the thirty minutes of outside exercise. When Eric joined us, I had to work around his asthma. He doesn't tolerate cold winds.

We loved the way he'd kick his little legs. Once he did his little performance when the schoolgirls were here. "Look," exclaimed one. "He's riding his bicycle! He's even hanging onto the handlebars!" And that explained it exactly. That is, if there's such a thing as riding a bike while sitting flat on the floor. I just never saw the like!

One hunting season we all had a break in our routine. We joined Allan's sister Edith and her family on their dairy farm for four days. Even though we didn't come back with any big buck stories to share, it was a delight to join in their everyday activities and see what others call normal. I wouldn't need to worry about my "going outside once a day" plan if I had Edith's lifestyle, but we each work with the circumstances we have.

I learned that when the babies sleep, even though the house is in need of dust cloth, broom, and scrub rags, those things wait while I write. A good day is when there are good things baking, like butter tarts and Dutch apple pie, while I take a break.

I recall the time Alyssa was two, almost three, and I actually managed to clean my messy, unorganized storeroom one day. Alyssa found her skates and proudly carried them downstairs. She laid them on the mat by the door and said, "I'll just set them here so Dad can take me skating on the river when he gets home."

Oh that I would have a little more of her spirit. Just a little more faith. Wait until Dad comes home. How does a two-year-old remember for a year that you skate on a river? Is it because her young mind is free from the clutter of worries and concerns?

So for us, February does not mean that we'll get rid of the winter woolies. Some years we have −19 degrees Celsius for the coldest day. (For my readers down south, that's −2 degrees Fahrenheit.) Another year it was −27 degrees Celsius.

The children and I don't venture out if the temperature dips that low. But on good days, we manage to get our daily fresh air and exercise. I bundle us up and wrap a long furry scarf around the baby's neck and cover his nose. Then he sits there, contentedly sucking his bottom lip and sniffing his scarf until the rest are ready to go.

• • •

Some of the families in the community have enjoyed a taste of caribou meat. Although caribou live in Canada, they are as rare as the polar bear here in southern Ontario. When they go for caribou, the hunters travel north until they reach the great caribou herds migrating from their northern tundra summer range to their forested, southern winter range. If the hunters had traveled south the same number of miles, they would have reached Florida! Yet they hadn't traveled to the top of Quebec; they went only about three-fourths of the way up, to where the road ran out.

It was fascinating to see the long, curving antlers of the caribou that friends brought back. They reminded me of thin moose antlers. The small horn sweeping from the base of the antler was a mystery, but I found out it works as an eye shield. The huge spreads belong to the bulls, while the females and smaller calves have smaller racks. The head is covered in soft, tight wool.

There's a look of longing in my hunter's eyes as he listens to our friends' stories. I hope that if he ever decides to go, he will take his wife along! Wouldn't that be something to see? They tell me that for the last twelve hours of the trip you drive through evergreen forests that don't have a chance to grow tall. The herd our friends hunted numbered over one million caribou. They aren't shy about humans and have only one thing in mind: get to their winter home.

Without winter, wouldn't we miss crunchy snow in the moonlight, the world covered in hoarfrost, glorious sunrises, and red-nosed children? Besides, when would I enjoy my lazy hobbies if it never got cold?

• • •

Spring is not my favorite season, but after a long winter each year, I'm convinced it is. To me, spring is freedom. Freedom from the cold, from the heavy winter wear, and from bundling the children. It's freedom from the house and the sewing machine. Freedom to come and go as you please.

When Eric was a toddler, I wondered how he would enjoy his first spring exploring the great outdoors on his own two legs. What would he do about the two roads just outside our front door? I knew Alyssa would continue to take her mothering duties seriously. I was frequently amused by things such as watching her at a quilting. She would mother the other children, keeping them all away from the top of the steps. Never mind that most of them were older than she was.

Before we moved to a bigger house, we had enough room for my husband, me, the two children, and all our needs, but not for many extras. So I always tried to find a spot for things, and would immediately sort my mail—tossing fliers and envelopes into the trash can and putting away the pieces I wanted to save.

One rare day Allan was at home and I was away when the mail lady came. That was the day we received a friendly letter from a reader of my column from Ohio. The woman who wrote it was hoping for a reply. I decided to write her back one night when the babies retired earlier than usual. All went well until it came to addressing the envelope. There was no address. I searched both sides of the letter in vain. Allan knew where it was.

"It's on the envelope," he said. "I think it was on the business card too."

"Business card?" I squawked.

"Didn't you see it? It had a nice picture of their lumberyard and their house across the way."

No, I didn't see it, and I didn't have to think where the envelope and business card might be. I knew they hit the garbage can soon after I came home. How could I have completely missed the business card?

The smirk on Allan's face and the twinkle in his eye kept me from telling him why I couldn't find it. As usual, I couldn't hold my tongue for too long though.

I used to have a directory that had most Amish names and addresses in it. When I houseclean, I like to use the rule "If you saved it for a year without using it, get rid of it." Well, that directory was bending the rules for years, so that fall I had pitched it.

I don't know why Allan thinks such things are so funny. Maybe because it's usually his things that I put in the garbage. Or maybe it's because I was having a hard time holding my temper. Eventually, I reached out through my column to the writer of the letter and she sent me her address. Again!

4

Too Much Time

NO MATTER WHAT DIFFERENCES we have in privileges and talents, we are all given the great gift of time. Sure, some have been given (or will be given) more time, but it really isn't important how much we have or will be given. What counts, of course, is what we do with it.

I wonder if the phrase "But I don't have enough time" isn't one of the more common ones in this land of plenty. So why do I utter this phrase? Yet I take time to grumble, to gossip, to be jealous, and to keep running when there are flowers to be smelled and all kinds of other time-consuming evils. Maybe I'd better stop and evaluate how I really am spending my precious gift of time. As the saying goes, "Yesterday is history. Tomorrow is a mystery. Today is a gift; that's why we call it the present."

Allan and I were reminded that maybe we use "But I don't have enough time" too often. One evening the neighbor boys came and coaxed Allan to go fishing with them.

"I have too much time," he teased them, when what he meant, of course, was that he didn't have time. After they left, Alyssa asked what the boys were doing.

"Going fishing," Allan told her. "Did you want to go too?"

"No," she shook her head.

We raised our eyebrows at each other. Normally she'll go anywhere simply for the sake of going away.

"I'm too busy!" she murmured under her breath.

That time has elapsed is very evident in our neighborhood. Across the way, in an old schoolhouse converted to a house, lived an older gentleman we knew. He eventually moved to a group home closer to where his daughter lives.

We have missed the courteous, intelligent neighbor puttering by in his silver Volkswagen. His gentle nature made it simple for him to live by the "Live and let live" motto. He carried insects from his house back to the great outdoors. The birds, snakes, and little animals found refuge in his garden. Sundays were for going to church. Hats were to be removed upon entering a home. Folks were politely addressed as mister or missus.

Everything he owned was in working order or being used. If not, it was fixed or given to someone who could use it. Truly, he made the neighborhood a better place.

During my schoolmarm years, I was privileged to be his housecleaner each Saturday. What a restful way to end a hectic week. One week he reminded me of the freedom we often take for granted. While living in France he also had a housecleaner. She had formerly cleaned house for a member of Hitler's army. One day in a fit of resentment she dropped a figurine of Hitler. The man she worked for then used the spurs of his boots to rake long, ugly gashes down her legs.

Across the corner, another house stands empty. My little ones adopted the mommy from that house; she moved in with Doddy Jantzis'. "Mommy Cathy" became Alyssa's best friend early on; Alyssa discusses many important things with her.

Mommy Cathy taught her about going to school, numbers, and poems and songs from her childhood days. They've long shared snacks and their favorite treat, candy. Dementia stole Mommy Cathy's memory but not her smile, chuckle, and pleasant disposition.

Up the road at Uncle Earl's, the *Dawdy Haus* stands empty. My Doddy Albrecht died in 2009. He was afflicted with Parkinson's disease for many years. Despite it all, he labored long at a history of Milverton Amish surnames. An elderly deacon recopied his notes, and they were recently published in a book titled *A Glimpse of Our Ancestors*.

And so pass the small moments of time and days into years—a great gift we've been given.

• • •

When autumn's inspirations have passed and cabin fever is a real thing, we all must go outside no matter how long it takes to get there, how many clothes we must layer on, or how little time we actually spend out there. We always return with a different attitude and a renewed appreciation for the four walls that shelter us and the Pioneer Maid they harbor.

Window washing is always one of my last jobs before the snow flies. It is almost as if I hope it will "winter in" before I get it done. But who wants to gaze at a peaceful snowy morn through windows speckled with fly dirt? So I reluctantly gather my bucket of vinegar water, the lime green window cloths, and my hoopster stepladder. Slowly I wind my way from window to window. First in the store, then the shop, and finally the house. They're all nice, modern windows that are easy to wash, and often the children provide me with entertainment lest I get bored. One year Eric took a tumble as I worked. That resulted in a bloody chipmunk cheek that totally changed his appearance for a few days. And only Alyssa (or her mother) could manage to climb down off the hoopster and land smack in a pail of vinegar water!

Eventually window washing is finished and the fly dirt disappears for another season.

5

Mothers Who Write

As I'VE GRADUALLY STEPPED into the writing world, I've enjoyed attending several meetings for writers from the plain community. The first was for writers and editors of *Plain Interests* magazine. Since this meeting was open to all, I decided to see for myself what professional writers and editors discuss.

We traveled an hour and a half to the Alymer community, where the meeting was held in a schoolhouse. The Alymer community publishes the Pathway magazines. We were treated to an English course by teacher Bert Farmwald, a gifted speaker. He kept the audience spellbound with twinkles in their eyes and grins on their faces throughout the sultry July afternoon. He claimed the human brain starts working as soon as you are born and doesn't stop until you stand up to speak to a crowd. Well, if his stopped, ours started.

Consider this: since June 2010 there are one million English words (according to the Global Language Monitor)! To think there are times when I still don't know what to write!

Edit yourself when you write. Ask, could someone take another meaning from this? Think about this:

The teacher from Canada read a book about an orphan.

The teacher read a book about an orphan from Canada.

The teacher read a book from Canada about an orphan.

Isn't it understandable that writers are often misunderstood? They aren't always saying what they mean. Sometimes they are, but the readers aren't reading it the way the writer is writing it.

One last point: we pay for our education now or later.

We had a superb lunch that day, all natural and organic. Sausage, ribs and pork, potato casserole, salads, and 100-percent whole wheat bread, topped off with ice cream made of sheep milk with strawberries and cake.

We witnessed history when senior editor David Wagler and his wife, Ida Mae, sang "The Story of the Titanic." Even their small great-grandchildren quietly listened to their Doddy's singing.

There were other great speakers and writers. I was grateful to be included, along with my grumpy little Eric. He cut his first tooth that day, so we were thankful my mother was along.

• • •

Another Saturday I was able to attend a writer's meeting for the *Connection*, a monthly magazine written by Amish and plain Mennonite writers. My monthly column, or "letter," in it is called Northern Reflections. Since it was a Saturday, Allan would be at home with the children. With Mommy's help, surely he'd do okay with the baby, too.

In the end, I took my thirdborn, a fourteen-month-old bundle of energy, along to that meeting. Mommy ended up needing to attend a funeral. I thought Allan's day might as well be more productive than simply babysitting, so I hinted,

"Wouldn't you be able to put the new cellar door in while you're in the house a lot anyway?"

The two oldest gleefully packed Mom's lunch. They lined up for their goodbye kiss before joyfully waving me off. Certainly a day with Dad looked promising.

It was a wonderful day. Baby and I sat at the back of the room listening to discussions like "Periods—the more the merrier." We learned how to get started with our writing and how to write correctly.

We ate our lunch and chatted with circle letter pals who would now be strangers no more. While my baby had his afternoon nap, I joined in the workshop. We need to tighten up our writing and keep it simple, I learned.

As we traveled home, I basked in the afterglow and mulled over my day. I reveled in the pleasant rolling scenery of Mennonite homesteads. As those slowly changed to Amish farms, my thoughts turned to home.

I wondered about my two little ones and their dad. I thought of the unfolded laundry and the jars of beef waiting to be carried down to the fruit cellar. The unswept floor and the dirty breakfast dishes crossed my mind too.

That was the sight that met me when I opened the door. That and a lot more.

There was dust everywhere, and the wall was gone! The one that divided the kitchen and the living room that we had talked of removing. It was a stunning combination. That wide-open space strewn with everything you can imagine, and covered with dust. In the midst were my two excited little ones and their dad. Excited to show Mom the surprise and disappointed that she had come home before they cleaned up the mess.

I did the only thing left to do. I exclaimed in delight at the wide-open space and made hot dogs for supper. I bathed my three little ones and tucked them into bed.

Then Allan and I met in our new living room/kitchen combination. We picked up, swept, wiped, and mopped till we felt the grit each time we blinked. With order restored, we knew a hot shower was the perfect way to end the perfectly wonderful day.

• • •

One woman wrote me a note mentioning how truly grateful she was for the opportunity to write for the publication who publishes her. She added, "As I'm sure *you* are by writing for the *Connection*." Truly grateful? Yes, I am. Grateful to write. Grateful for readers. And very grateful for editors who labor to publish my feeble words.

Somehow, I'm sure those editors have never absorbed my truly grateful feeling. Failure to meet deadlines and the guidelines I've ignored are sure to have any editor wondering about gratefulness. It's not my lack of appreciation that makes me tardy or send in less-than-desirable articles. It's the things that get between my pen and paper.

• • •

Having little ones certainly makes it hard to meet deadlines at times. Sometimes it is the store, and sometimes just plain tiredness.

All my good intentions have been grabbed, stomped on, and pitched into the dirt. One year it was December 14 and my monthly *Connection* letter was still sitting on my kitchen table. I still had one chance to get it to the *Connection* editors by the fifteenth, so I rushed it to town to the accountant's office to fax it. I hastily paid the fee and promised the woman behind the desk that I'd be back for my letter some other day. The days passed. The new year came before I finally walked back into that office. "But the letter didn't go through," the businesswoman explained. I gasped and sputtered, and went into a dither as we straightened things out. The dear *Connection* ladies received my letter that afternoon, almost one month after my good intentions.

Another time my good intentions for getting my letter sent were hit by the flu bug. It turned my children and me into a bunch of sniffling, sneezing, miserable humans with high fevers and no energy. We all longed to feel like Daddy, the faithful nurse! Eventually I got the letter mailed.

• • •

I usually didn't mind exposing our life to *Connection* readers. No one knew who I was anyway. Well, maybe some knew, but it was just my parents, their friends, some uncles, and Dad's employee. That was about it. But things started to change.

I began hearing comments on steps, on sidewalks, in kitchens and living rooms, or just about anywhere folks gathered. I began to feel intimidated, as if my pen were on a leash. Somehow I'm not quite as comfortable when familiar eyes read what I write. When visiting others in person, I am the other way around. I'm comfortable talking to those I know, and am shyer to speak up in front of strangers. Time to overcome my shyness.

My sister invited us over for supper one night a few years ago. "I invited you to tell you that you may not write about me in the *Connection*," she informed me. "Why, my whole tableful of guests last night were discussing what you wrote about me, and I had no idea what they were talking about."

Then I really felt on a leash . . .

• • •

Occasionally, when the timing is right, I take a little vacation right here at home. I write, read, and drink coffee, pretending to be completely ignorant of all the jobs staring me in the face. I know there's no need to feel guilty. We've all heard phrases like "If Mom ain't happy, ain't no one happy" and "Happy wife, happy life." After my mini vacation, my fatigue vanishes and I feel truly grateful for the waiting duties and the little facts that make them so demanding.

So the length and accuracy of my writing might depend more on how much "vacation time" I have than on anything else!

"Time flies" must be a worn-out phrase by now. However, I've found a way to make time fly even faster. When facing a deadline and seized by a case of writer's block, I use too many of my precious writing minutes to study a list of tips that are important stepping stones for writers. My pen just droops further.

• • •

Now I'm no longer a "new" writer. At least I don't feel that I am. Shouldn't attending the biannual *Connection* writers' reunion be a turning point? Before that day my husband and I hadn't met any of the *Connection* "family" in person (the *Connection* is based out of Topeka, Ind.), so we were really new. Though being new is a thrill, old is so much more comfortable.

We enjoyed traveling with both sets of parents and Uncle David. Sister Susan told me that that's a spoiled way to travel. Maybe that's why the children did so well? They had the grumps for a week after we got back, and guess who had to deal with them then!

Everyone was curious to know how long it took to drive from our far-off country. Six hours. Yes, that's it. That didn't include our stops, though. We only had birth certificates to cross the border, so we had a short stop there until the authorities had everything sorted out. We returned home after midnight Sunday morning. I felt like I was still holidaying when I woke from a late Sunday afternoon nap and sister Laura was sweeping the kitchen floor while sister Kathryn was busy cooking a meal "out of nothing."

Once again, I was so very grateful for willing helpers.

6

When Your Ears Are Too Long

I WAS HAVING ONE of those weeks. You know the kind: you just don't feel like pulling yourself out of bed, your daily work looks dull and monotonous, the children are grumpy, and you simply forget to count your blessings. I felt just like little P. J. Funnybunny in Alyssa's favorite book. He had too many brothers and sisters, hated to eat the cooked carrots his mother provided, and his ears were far too long. P. J. Funnybunny learned to bloom where he was planted by going on a foray with all kinds of other animals. He found out that the beavers didn't have it that nice, as they worked too hard. He got a headache when he hung upside down with the possums. The birds were okay until he tried to fly. Who wanted to sleep all winter with the bears? Of course, it didn't take long to find out that he didn't want to live with the skunks.

Well, I didn't want to be a P. J. so I just stayed home, feeling sorry for myself and thinking, "This too shall pass." It did, with a bang! Seemingly overnight, Eric got sick with pneumonia and chest infection and there I was sitting in a hospital room for three days. Suddenly I was overwhelmed with blessings! Why, even leaving the room was a wonderful, wonderful privilege, and grumpy children are much, much better than sick ones.

If you are tired of your big long ears, just be glad for them. At least then everyone knows you're a bunny.

When Eric was better again and the days grew shorter, we decided to change our schedule. Our shop work went better in the mornings when the babies were still sleeping.

One morning everyone was a little off track after a long weekend. First, Eric had a coughing fit from a spray Allan used.

Next came Alyssa. "Mom, Mom, here, have a piece of my blankie," she offered, trying to coax me into snuggling with her. "The kitty is dead," she stated after securely tucking a tiny piece of her beloved blankie under my cheek. "It's dead in the barn."

Alyssa had been enjoying the new litter of kittens so much, especially her favorite, Brian. But horses have no respect for a litter of kittens, and one by one they disappeared, much to Alyssa's disappointment.

To Alyssa's chagrin, I don't have many tender thoughts when it comes to fuzzy felines. "Just pet Brian a little, Mom," she had coaxed. "Don't you like him, Mom? Do you just like chickens? Just chickens, Mom?"

Sure, just chickens. But they are much better butchered and in the freezer.

One time the chickens got a *steak* supper. We were low on meat, so I was pleased to find a steak in the freezer hiding among the vegetables, fruit, and the last of the venison. I set it to cook while Alyssa and I went to the garden to fetch the potatoes. While I was out there, I thought I might as well pick the tomatoes. We got a big boxful. Next we pulled some spent cornstalks for the horses. You can guess that we *smelled* that steak before we got back to the house.

"Hmm, bacon" was Alyssa's comment as she vigorously chewed her supper that night.

"Yeah, sure, it was just bakin' a little bit too long," Allan chuckled.

So that's why the chickens enjoyed a steak meal.

• • •

We were in the hospital again. What a wonderful place to be when your baby is blue and white and as limp as a Raggedy Ann doll. I lost some of my appreciation (for the hospital) the next day, though, after Eric bounced back to his usual, happy, energetic self. He was just finding out that his twenty-six inches allowed him to peek into the fish tank when Mom and a dutiful nurse ended his freedom. I was certain we earned a ticket for home after he escaped his room.

"I will take no chances," the pediatrician announced. "You will stay for one more day."

I was a little perturbed, but I tried to console myself with my stack of reading material.

What was I reading? Overseas there are big hospitals where you must bring your own bandages and blankets. Where the spread of disease is more common than the cure. There is no money for hospitals, the magazine states, because military generals keep it for themselves.

Now I was the puppy with my tail between my legs. While I was praying the selfish prayer of "Please let me go home today," there were mothers longing for clean, well-equipped hospitals. Hospitals with doctors who won't take chances with little nine-month-old asthmatic boys. Hospitals—just like the one I didn't want to be in!

So we cherished the moments when our little boy got back to his usual self. He had the cutest way of showing happiness or excitement. He'd kick and kick his little legs, stop in mid-crawl, sit back on his bottom, and beat out a rhythm with his heels. When we held him, waving his feet was good enough. You had to beware of sticking your toes over the edge of the couch, though. That was the perfect level for him, and you'd be sure to feel his four brand-new teeth!

• • •

Sometimes what we want is right under our nose but we still can't see it. I always wanted a recliner. Our house isn't big enough for one, but I often longed for the comfort, and I thought that I could put up with its bulkiness. Then my sister came over and wondered why I kept the glider rocker in my upstairs bedroom. Good question. Now it's in the "recliner corner" and we all enjoy gliding back and forth on its comfy, navy cushions. Besides all that, it fits in our house!

• • •

For over two weeks, a virus sapped my energy and ability to properly care for my family. Often it rendered me too weak to even sweep my floors.

One morning when I was weary of feeling weary, I read this special little poem by an unknown poet.

Is it raining, little flower? Be glad of rain.
Too much sun will wither thee; 'twill shine again.

The sky is very black 'tis true,
But just behind it shines the blue.
Art thou weary, tender heart? Be glad of pain;
In sorrow the sweetest virtues grow as flowers in the rain.
God watches and thou wilt have sun.
When clouds their perfect work have done.

The clouds weren't pleasant, but they did their job. First of all, I have a much greater appreciation for my health, more sympathy for the suffering, and a greater awe of the marvelous way God created our bodies to heal themselves. All the kindnesses that were showered on me I longed to return. Maybe clouds are sunshine in disguise?

PART II

Winter Blows Cold

7

Thankful Hearts

ONCE AGAIN, late autumn speaks—urging us, warning us. Time is running out. Frosty days are just around the corner. Gather those apples, cabbages, pumpkins, and squash. Fill the woodshed. Stuff the cracks. Hurry, hurry through the golden autumn days.

Aunt Ann will be overjoyed when October 13 is here at last and it's her birthday! At my grandpa Albrecht's house, there was always Aunt Ann. Ann to color with, Ann to play Uno with, Ann to play soccer or school or whatever it was that we wanted to play. And it never changed. As we grew older and moved on to other interests, Ann's stayed the same. I remember when Mom explained that it was Down syndrome.

Aunt Ann now lives with Aunt Marion and Uncle Tom. All her brothers, sisters, nieces, nephews, and their children, the neighbors, and many others receive one of Ann's homemade birthday cards on their special day.

It's the time of year when I'm thankful for every stainless steel bowl, kettle, strainer, and canner we received on our wedding day. This season I am doubly thankful for every jar that's free of chips and cracks—and is in one piece—waiting to be filled.

One night I was jerked from dreamland by a crashing and banging and tinkling of glass. I was mumbling incoherently, but when my husband said the noise sounded like jars, I was suddenly wide awake. "It *is* jars!" I shrieked. "It's the old jar shelf beside the plumbing downstairs."

I tried not to use my imagination, and rolled over to finish my night's sleep. The morning light came soon enough to reveal what I had expected. The old, rotten, worm-eaten shelves that I'd loaded with my empty canning jars stood no more.

So my jar-buying days were a lot further from being over than I had thought. At least the jars were empty and I could salvage about half of them. I'm kicking myself still. After all, it was a preventable accident. When I asked my mother-in-law if I might use the shelves in our shared basement, I should've taken a warning from her answer: "I'm not sure they'll even hold empty jars."

I'm getting new canning shelves for my canned goods.

• • •

My sisters draw, paint, color, and craft like professionals. The artist's touch eludes me. Not completely, but almost.

That's why Alyssa was thrilled when she received a paint-by-number set as a gift, while I sighed. It was completely above her level: oil paints, hairline strokes, and mixing paint to create new shades. I feebly tried to dampen her excitement by telling her to wait until Aunt Laura could come over. But enthusiasm is contagious, so I read the instructions aloud. She gathered the supplies while I hunted for an extra brush. We swished, blended, and traded suggestions. It was surprisingly fun, but we found it takes a long time to do an oil painting even if you're using a fat Crayola brush. Frequently our painting got long periods of rest. Occasionally, though, when the other children slept, we painted some more.

When Aunt Laura came, Alyssa ran to show her our masterpiece.

"Who did that?" she asked. "It's pretty good."

There you go; if spring just doesn't come, maybe you should try something you know you can't do. If you're really sure you can't, find a five-year-old to help you. Then you can blame the splotches, the wrong colors, and the paint dots on your face and clothes on her. As they say, "If only the best singers would sing, the forest would be a quiet place."

8

No Sweeter Thing

For God so loved the world, that he gave his only be-
gotten Son, that whosoever believeth in him should not
perish, but have everlasting life.

—John 3:16

IT IS NO LONGER OTHERS' children I teach, but our own
little ones. At Christmas we especially want to teach them about
the Greatest of Gifts. As parents we want to renew our efforts to
live a life for Jesus, and to love our neighbors as ourselves.

At Christmastime we make sure we read Scripture aloud
from a children's Bible storybook:

God sent the angel Gabriel to visit Mary in the city of
Nazareth in Galilee. . . . "You will have a son, and you
will call him Jesus. He will be a King who will rule forever." . . . Mary and Joseph journeyed to Bethlehem to
obey the Roman emperor's command. . . . When they
reached Bethlehem it was crowded with people. . . . They
could only find the stable of an inn in which to rest. . . .
That night baby Jesus was born. . . . Mary wrapped him
in soft cloths called swaddling clothes, and laid him

in a manger. . . . Shepherds were watching their flocks that night near Bethlehem. . . . A great light shone. . . . Suddenly the angel of the Lord came near. "Fear not, for I bring you good tidings of great joy, which shall be to all people. For unto you is born this day in the city of David a Savior, which is Christ the Lord. And you shall find the baby wrapped in swaddling clothes, lying in a manger." . . . Many angels sang, "Glory to God in the highest, and on earth, peace, good will toward men." . . . The shepherds said, "Let us now go to Bethlehem, and see this thing which the Lord has made known to us."

We all sing together: "O Come All Ye Faithful"; "Away in a Manger"; "Joy to the World the Lord Is Come." Then, softly, "Stille Nacht, Heilige Nachte," before tucking everyone, droopy with sleep, into their beds.

What if no cold north wind howled around our house these dark winter evenings? What if it did and there were no woodpile stacked to the rafters? What if the fruit cellar and pantry were not stocked to overflowing and the closets stuffed with fleecy coats, caps, and blankets? What if we had never been taught to keep our homes and families near our hearts? What if no one had ever read us the wonderful story of our Savior's birth, nor shown us the way to him? What if we had never been taught to sing with a heart full of praise, "Glory to God in the highest?"

My heart is full of thank-yous:

Thank you that the promise of Christ's first coming is fulfilled.

Thank you for parents who led us in precious truths.
Thank you that we, as parents, were given these truths to
pass on.

Each year we all look forward to crowning the year with
a week of gatherings with family and friends. It feels good to
relax and leave the hustle, tensions, and troubles of the old year
behind. We begin the New Year with renewed spirit.

One year a friend sung a precious voicemail message: "When
it seems life's not fair and a burden we bear. Then just think of
our Lord on the cross . . ."

• • •

To me Christmas is family and food; Allan is usually home
for a week that starts with church on Christmas Day and is followed by gatherings, enjoying our Christmas cards and gifts,
singing the carols, catching up with reading and odd jobs, and
finally eating, and eating some more. We eat the traditional turkey and ham, dressing and rice, Jell-O salads, cutout cookies,
sweet squares, and candies and fruitcake. My mother thinks she
has to include "schnitz and gvetch." She sweetens a mixture of
stewed apples and plumped prunes—the schnitz and gvetch—
just the way her mother always did.

Allan's mom likes onion pie: chopped onions, cream, flour,
and celery seed in a piecrust served warm with the main course.
Oh, it's all good. Everything is good at Grandma's house!

As a teenager I'd make pounds of fudge, maple bonbons,
chocolate-covered caramels, toffee, and peppermint patties. I'd
sell most of them as fast as they were made and always had
a batch in preparation. During my early years of marriage I

realized how much time I spent making just one batch of candy. Besides time, there's the inconvenience of the candy the guests leave behind. That's when there is such a thing as too much chocolate.

So each year there are fewer and fewer holiday treats at our house. I rely on the grandmas to provide our fill, and maybe even share a few leftovers.

Except for cutout cookies. We always make a few batches of those. Toward the end of each year we dig out cookie cutters of trees, men and women, candy canes, angels, and stars. We mix vanilla and ginger and roll out dough. We're done when there's cookie dough and icing on everyone's hair, face, and clothes. Plus there's enough smeared on the table, chairs, and floor to make another tray of cookies. We're left with a wonderful pile of strange-looking cookie blobs, amply covered in icing and sprinkles. We all call them the best cookies we ever ate, and they never last more than a few days.

Now that Alyssa can read and do some cooking, I've added a few more treats to our list. It will be fun with more help to make and eat them. Alyssa can make her special "Twix bars" and that will be our homemade candy. (See p. 250–254 for all my family's favorite recipes.)

Now for some guests to sample our treats! Maybe we'll even serve them turkey. That is, if Eric will part with one of his pets.

• • •

When Alyssa was five she went to "Mommy Far Away" with her pitiful confession: she had no gift for her mom and dad. Mommy Far Away assured her that Mom and Dad would be happy with a good little girl and did not expect a gift from her.

But she persisted until Mommy promised a spot beside her on her next shopping trip.

Pondering and worrying about the perfect gift passed the days until the anticipated shopping trip. The end of it brought back our little girl brimming with excitement. The package tucked under her arm was a wonderful surprise that only her brothers were allowed to see.

"It's just a cup," Eric said disappointedly.

"But he may not tell you, Mom!" Alyssa wailed. "Oh, well he didn't tell you that there are birds on it," she added secretively.

The days before Christmas were for wrapping and rewrapping their precious gift. Then there was the tremendous decision of which cup should be Mom's and which would be just right for Dad.

"Do you forget what Eric told you the present is?" Alyssa frequently asked.

By Christmas Eve the excitement was hard to settle. "When we wake up," Alyssa informed her brothers, "we will give Mom and Dad their gift."

Eyes glowing, they hurried off to bed, leaving Mom and Dad to finish with their own surprises.

Early that Christmas morn, the creaks on the stairs were accompanied by glad, childlike voices singing, "Jingle bells, jingle bells, jingle all the way . . ."

"Open it, open it," they cried, thrusting the packages into our hands. "I'll bet you can't guess what it is!"

It wasn't "just a cup" as Eric had said. At least, not the usual, heavy pottery mug I had expected. The cup, nestled in paper, was thin and made of fine china with delicate black-and-white birdies stamped on it. It lay there, pure and whole, a meek survivor of bumps and bangs, wrapping and rewrapping. Dad had one just like mine. "But his birdie sticks his head up farther," Alyssa showed us.

The children beamed with joy as we admired our gifts, deeming them fit only for Sunday morning and special occasion coffee.

"But look, children!" their dad pointed to the table. With childlike squeals of delight, they forgot the cups as they ran to admire their own surprises.

• • •

In January it will be time to pack Dad's lunch box again. Once more the children will flock by on their way to school. We will put away the Christmas treats and get out sewing projects. It will be time to do some inventory and year-end bookwork. Christmas will only be pleasant memories to warm us during January's cold blasts.

I will slowly leaf through our basket of Christmas cards, savoring each one again, and thinking of friends and family who sent them. We'll admire the pictures and copy some verses before storing them for crafts next season.

We will choose a new calendar for the kitchen. It must be carefully chosen, as it has many purposes. Its pictures must add charm to our favorite room. Inspiring verses are a plus. It will be filled with birthdays of family and friends, appointments, and notices. The margins will soon have lists of cards and letters to send. So we ask for a lot: big, beautiful, and inspirational.

Now we're ready for a brand-new year.

9

Winter Grows Old

I WAS HAPPY TO SEE yellow sunshine splashed across the dull browns, grays, and whites. My suggestion of a walk along the stream with the children brought immediate action. Coats, caps, and mittens were haphazardly pulled on and feet stomped into boots before they dashed outside. Our stream is just a glorified drainage ditch. It does have one well-worn horse trail running beside it that is perfect for walks. We saw that Peter Cottontail also used the trail, and we found his front door under the brush pile. Up, up in the blue, a jet roared.

By and by, duties clouded the beauty and I started the trek back to the buildings. My little ones followed, with Eric at the tail end as usual. "Mother duck leads the way and all her babies waddle after," he chuckled.

March seldom lets us see the last of winter, but it breathes promises of spring!

• • •

We had an inspiring visit to check out school for Alyssa. Rows and rows of quiet, studious students headed by three industrious teachers thrilled me. My children were equally impressed by the row upon row of bright cups on the wall beside the water tap. Thirst prevailed.

One night it was warm enough to wander across the pasture and sit on the riverbank. Silence reigned. Even the little ones had nothing to say until we stood up to go home. Alyssa flopped right down again. "Let's sit here again," she begged.

On another day, on our walk home from my sister Susan's place, Alyssa noticed that neighbor Dorothy's windows were really clean. Most of mine still wore their coat of winter grime. That inspired me to write, instead!

• • •

One day we were like the children in Dr. Seuss's *The Cat in the Hat* who thought it was too wet and cold so they sat inside and did nothing.

I mean, we *felt* like doing nothing at all. We wanted warm spring breezes and sunshine. We wanted to run outside, shed our woolens, plant seeds, and mow lawn. One customer commented, "The problem lies in our *ungeduld* [impatience]."

I reluctantly sorted laundry with the raindrops spitting against the pane. Then, though I didn't deserve it, a spring breeze blew the clouds away and the sun peeped through. I thoroughly savored the feel of my freshly dried, windblown laundry, ready for the drawers!

• • •

Later that week, I breathed deeply and reveled in a beautiful morning. The vehicles hummed by on the pavement, the sun burned the mist off the river, and the birds busily ate breakfast. The cookstove's ashes were cold, so I cooked our porridge and coffee on the gas stove. The heavens finally ceased their weeping. It was a day to rejoice, to seek forgiveness for our whining and gather strength to begin anew.

10

Sewing with Glue

WHEN "SUPERSTORM" SANDY came puffing up the east coast of North America and into our area on her last legs, day after day she dumped rain. Rain, rain, and more rain. The boys didn't mind. They were content on the floor with their tractors, blocks, and animals. Each took a long nap.

For Alyssa it was a different story. She wasn't a baby who needed naps anymore. In her preschool years, she needed constructive things to do. Her days grew long. Maybe a little boring. Sometimes undesirable behavior erupted.

One day she saved herself. "Remember that book of things to make, Mom? You said we'd look at it someday when it rained."

Yes, I remembered my thrift store find. It was titled *Surviving Your Preschooler: A Mother's Manual*. Just what we needed. So with a dozen jobs staring at us, we sat down to browse through the book. With 365 different ideas, surely we'd find one that would work.

Circle Bears appealed to this mom with no crafting skills. So away we went, with Eric pitching in. We gathered construction paper, scissors, glue, and crayons. We traced around a large bowl to make the bear's tummy. A medium-sized bowl made its head. We traced around a small glass to make four paws. Two half circles formed the ears. The book suggested cutting out smaller white circles to glue onto the paws, tummy, and ears. By the time we had everything cut out and glued, things were dragging a little, so we skipped that part. Last of all I showed her how to color in facial features.

After we finished Alyssa scrutinized the two creations carefully. "They're not the same," she noticed.

No, they weren't. Mom had made Eric's bear, with him helping whenever possible. Alyssa had made her own bear, with me giving as little assistance as possible, just as the book suggested. This was new for her. Usually little brother cannot equal or best her.

Later, I had a chance to read the first chapter of the book. The chapter just for moms. It conveyed the idea that if your normally sweet-tempered child becomes moody and hard to deal with, there's a good chance she's just plain bored. I wasn't sure boredom was good grounds on which to blame bad behavior.

Then something happened to change my mind. On the sixth rainy day in a row, Alyssa was scheduled for a dentist appointment. There's nothing fun about filling two cavities. The outing was medicine for her attitude though. And I kept our *Surviving Your Preschooler* book handy for the long winter months.

When we find a new *Connection* in our mailbox, the children always insist that I read the children's story aloud. Next it's *Through the Eyes of a Child*. Sometimes even *Fins and Feathers*. When they pass my column, *Northern Reflections*, one of them will be sure to comment, "There's Mom's page." None of them ever had any idea what it said. One day I changed that after I tired of reading the same pages over and over.

"Let's read Mom's page," I suggested. They listened very quietly until I read of Alyssa letting her boots get baled into the hay. "I didn't know you would do that, Mom," she said in a very quiet voice, regarding me telling her story. They never asked me to read Mom's page again.

I also read them the Laura Ingalls Wilder books. I figured the books might be over their heads. I needn't have worried. Alyssa lives in a "Laura and Mary" world. Even Eric shouts out answers when I pop a few questions. Best of all is when Dad sits down to read a chapter.

• • •

Alyssa's eyes sparkle when she talks of our friends' little girl, Darla Jo, who is almost her twin. The day after Alyssa's fifth birthday, Darla Jo would be five too—a little girlie who likes kittens and ponies and lives far away in Indiana.

On another day, baby Kyle learned the meaning of what was on the other side of the door that divides our part of the house from Mommy and Doddy Jantzi's. There were hugs and cuddles, treats, and plenty of attention from Mommy and Doddy and Uncle David. At ten months old he learned to bang on the door and call hopefully. After that he often watched for his chance to quickly slip over.

• • •

One day when we were all bored, I promised the children we'd make a craft after Eric woke from his nap.

"Let's make it now," Alyssa begged. "Eric, do you want to make a craft before or after your nap?" she haggled.

The reply was swift and sure. "Oh, before my nap I'll make my *crack*."

For the *craft* we decorated empty coffee cans. You may cover it with construction, wrapping, or plain paper before decorating it. We just peeled off the labels and glued on seed catalog flower pictures, plus stickers. Alyssa printed her name on hers. Now they had pretty cans to store crayons, play dough, socks, or treasures.

Play this game with your preschooler: Lay a number of objects on the table. Remove one while your child covers her eyes. Can she think of the object that is missing?

• • •

I'm still trying to master my sewing machine. I'm happy when my sewing machine is purring just fine and not pulling some of the stunts it's known for. "It's not the machine, it's *you*," my sisters say. I'm sure they're right. The machine is as good as new.

It's just that when I sew, nothing runs slick and smoothly. I always say, "Now I know how some of my pupils had it." You try and try. You work much harder than anyone else does, but the end results are far from superior. You must not give up, and its funny how there is satisfaction in not giving up.

As the children get older, sewing goes better. There are fewer interruptions with Alyssa old enough to entertain the others. There's always "practice makes perfect." Not perfect, maybe, but better. My favorite improvement comes from the tip I gleaned: "Look twice. Sew once." It eliminates the frustration of having to use my seam ripper and wasting so many precious minutes.

• • •

On a morning when hoarfrost dazzled our world, the children and I clopped down the road with our horse, Mabel, to a quilting. It gave Alyssa the perfect idea. She would make her grandma Jantzi, "Mommy Over There," a beautiful quilt to thank her for the doll clothes she had made for her.

"It will be the perfect gift," she sighed as she planned. She told me which hunk of material she'd like to use and that I must put it in a quilt frame for her.

After much explaining and convincing she settled for a dresser scarf. We cut a piece of material to size, plus another for her brother, who also wanted to "knit."

With Mom's little pink sewing basket full of supplies, and Mom to thread and knot, Alyssa set to work. Diligently, one stitch at a time, she stitched around the scarf. Early the next morning she stitched some more until finally she could present the wonderful surprise to Mommy Over There.

Little brother's project did not fare so well. The thread he brought to be threaded was longer than I was!

"I'm going to get done fast!" he chuckled.

He did, too. Within minutes thread and cloth were in a terrible tangle. Just as quickly, the project was abandoned for tractors and toy animals.

• • •

I don't read many books anymore. I still read, but magazines lend themselves better to reading with little ones in the house. It's easier to pick them up for a few precious minutes of reading, and they aren't as difficult to set down when it's time to get back to work. But when the weather gets nasty and the pace slows, it just feels as if you need a book in your hand. One book was especially good to pick up: *One Woman Against the Reich* is about a simple German housewife who kept her faith and helped her family keep theirs. Those were the days when Christianity was outlawed, ridiculed, and persecuted. In the end she won, not Hitler. Just the story we need for today's times, with the title changed to *One Woman Against the World*.

• • •

Growing flowers changes, too, with little ones around. The summer Eric was one year old, my beautiful, orange border lilies didn't bloom. Growing beside the sidewalk, they were all loaded with buds simply begging to be picked. The year before that it was Alyssa's "job." I have a hard time scolding because I remember doing the same thing to my mother's lily beds. Imagine! But now her yard blooms with lilies from spring till fall, so perhaps I'll have my turn yet too.

• • •

Sometimes other behaviors escape our notice as parents. At Eric's eighteen-month appointment for shots and a checkup, the doctor seemed to do an extra good job of checking his ears.

Finally he asked, "Has your baby been extra fussy lately?"

"Well, yes," I replied, "but I'm sure he's cutting his eyeteeth." Mothers always know.

"Does he pull at his ears?"

"Well, sometimes, I guess."

"What about his sleeping habits. Have they changed recently?"

"Oh, I guess he did wake up crying after he fell asleep last night, which is very unusual for him."

"Yes, yes," the doctor nodded. "Well, he has an ear infection, so no shots today. He'll need a light dose of antibiotics."

Duh, Mom. And this came only a week after I told my mother and Aunt Sarah that my children don't get earaches.

11

Not like Mom's

I WAS BAKING A PUMPKIN PIE. It was easy, using frozen crust left over from when my mother was here baking pie. That crust rolled out like a dream. It wasn't too sticky. Neither was it dry and crumbly. Just perfect. It would taste that way too.

My sister told me her husband asked why her pie doesn't taste like his mom's. She told him, "Because it tastes like Jarred's mom's." Jarred is their son. "Besides that," she said to me, "it doesn't even taste like my mom's."

Sigh . . . maybe someday we'll perfect the art.

• • •

One morning Eric was busy with his breakfast of scrambled eggs, toast, and chocolate milk. Suddenly a piece of breakfast went sailing to the floor.

"Eric," I said reprovingly, "what was that?"

"Oh," came his reply, "a chicken bone."

My *Taste of Home* cookbook that my mother gave me for Christmas sure helps beat midwinter cooking blahs. You don't even have to read the recipe—to see if it'd be good, you just look at the picture. They all look delicious! I took a shine to the peanut butter sandwich cookies. They looked a little complicated to make with the assistance of my two helpers, but I couldn't refuse. So we got the cookies mixed, even with gobs of dough disappearing from the ends of little fingers. It was worth it. Partly because they were so good. Partly because my helpers were so excited to present them to Dad and tell him about stirring sugar, eggs, and flour and even about the "picking" (snacking on the dough). I guess it was okay for once that we didn't have much of an appetite for supper, because we had all been nibbling on the end results. Everyone had appetite for another *cookie*, though!

• • •

I'm a procrastinator. That is, I used to be a procrastinator. I've been trying to change my habit ever since I stumbled across an article in an old *Reader's Digest*. The article described procrastination as the art of keeping up with yesterday. It further claimed that it can take years off a person's life. It saps energy, motion, and time. Worse is that the fears, self-doubts, and low tolerance for the unpleasant which are part of the procrastination pattern can lead to alcoholism, anxiety, and depression. Also, isn't procrastination just sloppy time management or plain old laziness?

I wasn't so sure what to think of such strong statements, but they were enough to get me thinking of all the things I was procrastinating on. I also enjoyed the solution it offered. It suggested trying the Swiss cheese approach: Instead of doing the project in one chunk, try poking holes in it. With whatever time you have, do one small part of the overall task.

I tried it with organizing the filing cabinet. I finished after two days. Next came the cooking utensil drawer. After buying drawer organizers at the dollar store, I had that jumble organized in a few minutes!

During all this organizing, I'd still been procrastinating. It was about the junk drawer. It was far more junky than most junk drawers because we'd been filling it up since we moved. Most of the items in it had no home. I thought of those awful procrastination side effects (saps energy and time), and one day I poked a hole. I let Alyssa empty the contents of that drawer. Three days later I was still boiling used snap lids in vinegar to clean them. That drawer had been full of them.

Now the junk drawer no longer exists. We're storing our Saran wrap, tinfoil, and sandwich bags there, so there's no danger of procrastinating about the junk drawer again.

Maybe someday I'll be completely free of this habit.

• • •

All the children want for breakfast these days are egg sandwiches. And ketchup. Egg sandwiches to dip in ketchup. What do you think of when you hear "egg sandwiches"?

Before we were married, Allan would say that all he could cook were egg sandwiches and canned soup. I always wondered what he meant, but never asked. Egg sandwiches to me were cold, hard-cooked eggs mashed with mayo, salt, and pepper, and spread between bread slices. I considered that quite a procedure for a man who "couldn't cook."

After our marriage, I found out what Allan meant by egg sandwiches. One Sunday morning, while I prepared for church, he pulled out the bread, eggs, butter, and fry pan. Each slice of bread had a yolk-sized hole pulled from its middle before it was flopped into the buttered fry pan. The egg was broken carefully over this hole, and its yolk burst. A sprinkle of pepper and salt and a few minutes of frying on each side was all it took. Our breakfast was a delicious egg sandwich. "Egg-in-the-middle" was what we had always called it at home. I usually take over the making of the egg sandwiches these days. Everyone cheers when Dad occasionally reaches for the fry pan, though. They're so much more delicious.

We're eating local honey—very local honey. Our nieces have two hives, and they are eagerly learning everything about keeping bees. Honey tastes so much sweeter when it's made from the neighbor's flowers. Maybe even our flowers.

• • •

For a wedding gift, my aunt presented us with a cast-iron fry pan. Despite being new, shiny and silver-colored, it was still the same awkward heavy skillet, just like the one Mom had used for years. I shoved it to the darkest corner of my cupboard and gave the stainless steel fry pan with nonstick Teflon coating first place. It worked wonderfully. Nothing would stick. It was light and easy to handle and heated up quickly. I was convinced that I'd never need my cast-iron pan.

That was until the Teflon coating on my favorite pan started to scratch. Next, things started to stick a little in the middle, where most of the scratches were. Then I read a strange story of a woman who was using a secondhand Teflon-coated pan in her tiny apartment kitchen. When her canary mysteriously died, she wondered about the cause of its death and took it to the vet. The vet determined it died of poisoning; he blamed the Teflon pan.

Really? Well, my pan wasn't performing very well anyway, so I dragged my iron pan out. I greased it, heated it, and got it ready for use. The more I used it, the smoother its bottom got. It turned black like my mother's. It worked better yet when I remembered some important things about these ancient skillets. Preheating them makes them nonstick. It takes a while, I know, but I keep our pans on the lower back shelf of the Pioneer Maid so they're always warm and ready to go. In summer the gas stove heats the cast-iron pan quickly. After using, if you wipe the pan while it's still warm, it'll be ready to go in a few minutes. If you forget to wipe it while it's still warm, put a little warm water in the pan. Heat it till the water simmers. Scrape clean and wipe.

Oh, the naysayers will tell you of the food particles that remain and contaminate your pan. I like to think high heat kills any germs clinging to the bottom. As for the heaviness, I gladly accept any inconvenience for the experience of cooking just like the generations before me—and passing it on.

Passing on new skills has grown as Alyssa has gotten older. Chopping a bowlful of salad for supper became a great delight. Mixing cookies, cakes, and rolling piecrusts makes her feel grown-up and important. She dug the tomato holes in the garden. Then she put water in the holes, planted the tomatoes, and packed the soil firmly around the roots. Ready for Mom to put the frost and wind covers on. Next she planted peppers, celery, red and green cabbage, kohlrabi, and head lettuce.

· · ·

Howling winds and driving snow urge me to pull out mixing bowls and the ingredients for my favorite comfort foods. Sink your teeth into some cinnamon buns or juicy apple pie and all is well. Especially if you wash it down with some strong black coffee.

To me there is only one way to make a good apple pie. Just the way my mother does, of course! After you've lined the pan with crust, you mix half a cup of white sugar and another half of brown sugar with two tablespoons of flour. Make them heaping if you're using juicy apples. Cut two tablespoons of butter into the sugars and flour. Sprinkle some of this mixture onto the crust. Layer the pie shell with peeled, sliced apples before you sprinkle the leftover mixture on top, and pour two tablespoons of milk or cream over all. Finish with a dash of cinnamon and you'll have the best pie you've ever tasted.

I can just see all the shaking heads. "No, no, not like that," you are saying. "That is not the way to do it. Here's how."

. . . so many ways to do things.

While I was visiting my cousin she asked me to mix a batch of cinnamon buns. After the dough had reached new heights I rolled it to the usual half-inch thickness, and as usual I sprinkled it with cinnamon and sugar before rolling it into a long, fat roll. She leaned close, watching every move.

"What?" I asked. "Am I not doing it right?"

"Oh, I'm sure," she figured. "It's just I always divide my dough in half, then I roll it very thin before I make my roll."

Next she taught me to cook a delicious sauce to spread on the bottom of her roll pans. You don't need icing on top then. Later she confirmed that the rolls were fine despite her earlier misgiving when she saw my fat roll! So once more we proved that there's more than one way "to skin a cat" (wherever that comes from?).

Later I learned that there's more than one way for yeast to smell. Yes, you read right—yeast. All my life I was used to some form of Fleischmann's yeast. It has a strong, slightly sour, yeasty smell. At least that's what I thought was a yeasty smell, until Kyle took things into his own hands.

While we were shopping at a different bulk food store than we normally do, I was engrossed with the products in front of me. Kyle reached over the cart and plunked a container of yeast on the ground. The lid flew open and half the yeast spilled onto the floor. That's why yeast was added to my bill whether I wanted it or not. The next time I craved cinnamon buns, I decided to try the new yeast. What a delightful surprise when I added the yeast to the lukewarm water to soak. No strong smell arose; just a mildly pleasant odor. The buns were delicious and I briefly wondered if I should thank Kyle for his mischief. Time will tell. Maybe I'll be pulled back to the strong, sour, yeasty smell of yesterday.

I practice with yeast, fiddle with pies, and bake mountains of cookies. Never ask me for cake, though. They always look wonderful until I take them from the oven; then they slowly sink before my eyes.

"Bake them longer," Mom advised. Even though I bake them after the toothpick comes out clean, the same thing happens.

Once when I had more eggs than I knew what to do with, I tried an angel food cake. Surprise of all surprises, it was perfect! I congratulated myself. I could now bake cakes. I was sure of it. Of all cakes, angel food cakes would be the test. I was wrong again.

"Mom doesn't bake many cakes," Eric once told our hosts as they served cake. "I like cakes," he added somberly.

• • •

I was reading an article about baking bread; the writer mentioned that her husband had carved her a bread spoon. I read on, intrigued. A bread spoon? Who ever heard of such a thing, and what could its purpose be?

The husband had carved it from a piece of soft maple a little over twelve inches long. It gently curved outward to an almost-flat bowl a little more than three inches wide, somewhat like a paddle. Its shape worked very well in beating together bread ingredients.

So that's what it was! That "odd-shaped wooden spoon we received as a wedding gift." It's always what I grab to mix buns, rolls, and the occasional doughnuts. A bread paddle, no less! No wonder it works so well. Then again, maybe it's not. Maybe I'm guessing wrong. I've done that before.

12

A Bubble of Paradise

OUR CHILDREN WOULD LIKE a dairy farm. I mentioned to our neighbors that I thought we could have at least a few chickens. Unexpectedly, the neighbors came and said there were six chickens available now. I wasn't sure what to do. What would Allan say? Finally, I agreed to take them if they would house them for a few more days until we could get a cage ready. The children danced with excitement.

A few hours later a smiling face peeped in the door. "Your chickens are here," a small voice announced. A quick peek out the window showed me. There they were. A chicken in each hand of a straggling line of four boys! There were even two extra chickens for good measure. "Yes, yes!" our children cheered, but I had to send them home again. No cage, no feed. So the chickens walked back down the road again, in the hands of the four boys.

Finally the cage was built and Uncle Ken sent some laying mash over and we were all set. The first morning Alyssa was up before the sun to gather the eggs! The death of one chicken had Eric in tears, but Alyssa reassured him, "It'll still lay us eggs." Chicken ownership was a new thing for Alyssa. The remaining seven have been wonderful chickens.

• • •

A shoe salesman told me that the most beautiful part of the world is about a half-day's drive north of here. "The mountains don't compare," he declared. Dad says his neighbor took Swiss visitors up that way and they were equally impressed. Ah, I suppose it might be. Too close to home, I guess, to fully appreciate the scenery.

The previously mentioned salesman was trying to explain to me that my lifestyle and little corner of the world are not real. "You're living in a bubble," he explained.

I had to agree, because of what I told Allan after we returned from our shoe-buying venture in Toronto: "That life isn't real. Even the people aren't real."

I am so thankful I live in a bubble.

• • •

As a mother of little ones, a spotless room, or a quiet moment, is very precious. I cherish each of those moments whenever they unexpectedly come. Then I remember that, all too soon, my rooms might be too spotless and the quiet moments too long. That's when I go back to cherishing the chatter, the chubby cheeks, and even the clutter on the floor.

One day when Alyssa was four, she took a piece of wood and a piece of foam and nailed an old tea towel over everything. She even pounded the nails in by herself. In the end she called it perfect and presented her gift to her dad for his thirtieth birthday. He wasn't sure what the gift was. I think I'll just call the gift "love." Love from a four-year-old for her dad.

Eric was excited. Dad held a completely full bag of Jujubes, and the children were ready to share a treat. When Dad opened the bag, the unthinkable happened. Jujubes rained everywhere. Eric stood, awestruck, before he danced around and shouted, "It's a mess; it's a mess! It's a candy mess!"

Kyle paid no attention to the screeching. He sat in the middle of it, stuffing Jujubes into his mouth.

• • •

Our boys were close enough in size that people were often confused about who the big boy in our family was and who the younger one was. Part of it was Kyle's attitude from little and up. He proved "Where there's a will, there's a way." There wasn't much difference in size, unless Dad made a mistake with their pants. Then we were surprised how many inches of big Eric showed under Kyle's pants.

Kyle was outside every possible minute. We were grateful for Doddys' and Uncle David's help to guard him from the busy intersection. When they built up the road before paving it, I didn't like the feeling of living in a hollow. But it was a blessing. Climbing the ridge to the road was usually enough to change Kyle's mind, and he would come back to smoother territory.

PART III

Pajama-Clad Little Ones

13

A Small World

THERE'S NO DOUBT that those living on other continents don't have the same lifestyle we do. We've all read too much or seen too many pictures. It's closer to home that I get stuck in my own little world. Subconsciously, I'm sure everyone is living in a world like mine, forgetting that the climate changes lifestyles, work, and even the food we eat. The differences are made real through letters I receive from friends and readers, known and unknown.

A lady from Delaware wrote, "It's getting warm. Already, I'm looking forward to fall and winter. I don't enjoy summer all that much."

What! Looking forward to fall, in June! Why, we've only packed away our warm coats. I love the line "What is so rare as a day in June?"

A Kentucky friend writes, "Surely these words were penned by a northerner." I've never questioned them, so I suppose she could be right.

• • •

You never know what children are thinking but it's nice when they can let you know. Eric treasured each card that arrived on his third birthday. But there was one card that received the majority of his attention. Neighbor Andrew had made it. Inside there was a picture of a small boy and his dog roasting wieners over a campfire. Beside that were stamped wolves in a pine forest. Underneath, in grade-one scrawl, Andrew had printed "Eric and George." Eric was intrigued. He studied and studied those pictures. Finally, in a small, still voice he asked, "Why me and George so lonely in that big woods?"

• • •

Reading is my mental therapy. It keeps me grounded. As I mentioned, I used to read books. These days they take too much concentration and time. I sit there and read, oblivious to all the tasks and the arguing children. So I mainly stick to short magazine stories. Most of these are written by our people, for our people, of our people. That's okay, but a line from bygone summer teachers' training resurfaces for me: "Remember to read material that will stretch your minds."

Maybe that's the reason we've subscribed to the *Canadian Geographic*. With our latest issue we were educated in northern life and living. The far Far North. Far enough north to be the Arctic Circle.

There were photos of nomadic reindeer herders, crowds of penguins, and stunning icebergs. The gem among the photos is that of a little girl in her bare playground. There are swing sets and a dusting of snow, but that's all. Behind the playground stand small, brightly painted houses. Beyond them are bare hills. Frequently I scrutinize that picture. I wonder about the mothers who raise their children in such a stark, raw land. Then I know how Eric feels. There's loneliness in the picture.

We're a typical North American family. Our house is stuffed with too many things. And as in most houses, there's a mom who's supposed to know where everything is.

"Mom, where are my suspenders?" "Mom, my mitt. Did you see my mitt?" "Mom, Mom, Mom, my crayons . . . ?"

I was ready to relax on a Sunday morning. Maybe that's why I inwardly fumed, "Look for yourself," when Allan asked where the December issue of *Connection* was. I stomped over to the newspaper rack and triumphantly pulled the *Connection* from it. With a flourish, I proceeded to hand it over, then stopped short. Some air left my fully billowed sails as I stared at the August issue.

Try again. After all, it had to be in that rack somewhere. Search though I did, the missing periodical was not to be found. I searched all the usual spots—the bookshelves, the countertop, and under the couches. I tried to ignore my grinning husband as I searched the not so usual places. Finally, I gave up and silently huddled on my recliner in the living room to read. Allan good-naturedly moved his glider over to join me. What? There it was, neatly stuffed behind the glider's cushion. Even moms don't always know where everything is.

• • •

When they chorus, "Sing, Mom," we generally start with a new favorite. "We're on our way, we're on our way, on our way to Grandpa's farm" (repeat). "On Grandpa's farm, there is a _____ . The _____ , it makes a noise like this: _____ ."

The blanks were originally filled in with phrases like "black-and-white cow" or "white, wooly sheep." Lately we're being more original. Besides, there are no cows and sheep on our grandpa's farm. So we sing things like "On Grandpa's farm, there is a bobwhite quail," "a ring-necked pheasant," or "a colored mallard duck." The words vary with the changing pets at Grandpa's farm.

I think I've discovered the reason the boys around there want everything in a cage. Eric has caught the fever.

"Uncle Jody is my best friend 'cause him have lots of pets." Eric's eyes sparkled and danced just thinking of it.

More recently it's changed to begging. "Dad, when can I have pets like Uncle Jody?"

• • •

In Toronto, Ontario's capital city, we were strangers among strangers engaged in the business of buying shoes or selling them. His shoes weren't our style so we reluctantly walked over to answer his call. "Hello, hello! Are you Amish?" he was wondering. At our nod, he chuckled with delight. "I'm from Lancaster County, Pennsylvania. In fact, I own a farm adjoining an Amish farmer's. He milks his cows in my barn and works my fields. I didn't know there were Amish in Canada. But when I saw you I just knew I had to talk with you."

It's a small world after all . . .

We are just people living among people.

In 1 Corinthians 12, I read: "Now there are diversities of gifts, but the same Spirit. And there are differences of administrations, but the same Lord. And there are diversities of operations, but it is the same God which worketh all in all."

Oh, that we keep this in our hearts and learn to care more deeply for one another. Weep with the sorrowing; rejoice with those rejoicing. Kindness speaks so loudly. We should delight more in one another, considering each better than ourselves, especially our fellow church members.

The same moon and sun shine over us all. Ultimately, above all, the same Lord and Savior . . . the very one who said he sees each sparrow fall and can count every hair on our head.

• • •

I knew she was coming. My friend sent a message a few weeks earlier saying that our writer friend from Michigan would be in the area. I thought about it on Tuesday. By Wednesday it fled my memory. I was sure I had to get my cupboards cleaned before the spring rush in the store. Plus there was laundry to fold and the cookie jar was empty.

Thursday dawned with the usual morning rush. Shop work to do, lunch to pack, and breakfast to make. As soon as we waved Allan off, there were the children to dress, a circle letter to write, and a shoe order to phone in. It was just after I got in from the phone that there was a knock on the door.

The lady on the other side was a stranger. I assumed she wanted the store. "Hello," I greeted her. "Are you here for the store?"

"Well," the lady answered, "I wasn't sure where to go."

That was typical for new customers.

"Just a minute," I said, grabbing my boots. "I'll show you."

"Is that where she is?" the lady said when she could squeeze a word in. "I didn't know where I'd find Marianne. I hoped to meet her, as I'm her circle pal from Michigan. Or are *you* Marianne?"

The look on my face must have said it all. I shifted gears. Hard. I invited her in and we enjoyed a short, sweet visit while our sons played with tractors on the floor. Of course I forgot everything I meant to ask her or tell her until after she left.

And she saw us just how we are. Half past nine with breakfast dishes on the counter, unswept floors, and Alyssa's fuzzy braids. I didn't even have time for butterflies, so maybe she saw me just how I am too.

When I told Allan the story he asked, "Well, did you tell her what was wrong with you?"

"What was?" I wondered. How could I have forgotten that important visitor?

• • •

In a house with preschoolers, it's all about little things; little people with all their needs and even littler progress. Only a little work gets done between little interruptions. Then there are all the little things that are so important to little ones. Of course it takes more than a little time to answer all the little questions. Little by little, our day slips by with little being accomplished. Finally even our world feels very little and unimportant.

But some wise soul wrote, "Think naught a trifle, though it small appears; sands make the mountain, moments make the year, and trifles—life."

As the song we used to sing at school says, "And the little moments, humble though they be, make the mighty ages, of eternity."

Big swiftly lost its appeal the day I went big-city shopping for the store. The endless rows of houses crammed together before the congested streets held little charm. I turned west eagerly. Back to my little world that the salesman told me is not real.

One day of accomplishing big things was enough. Gladly, I was back to my "line upon line, precept upon precept" duties. Back to the little golden moments stuck together to form a wonderful day.

14

Listen to Me

I OFTEN THINK ABOUT IT. I even thought it would make a good article. So one morning I started. "Listening," I wrote at the top of a page. That's as far as I got. I left the rest of the page unblemished and went off to my mothering duties.

Listening. It's not something I'm qualified to write about, because I'm not a listener. I'm the talker. Although I'm the one eagerly nodding her head, I'm only partially listening to the speaker; I'm getting ready to spout out my idea or advice as soon as he's had his say, and sometimes even before. Then before I know it, I dominate the party. Again.

Then there are the children. They chatter on and on. I think my own thoughts and add the occasional uh-huh.

"Mom, listen," they demand.

"I am," I insist.

"No, Mom, look at me," they beg.

They want me to listen with my eyes and to really know what they are saying. They don't even need a response. They only want me to listen.

A friend from my teaching days once told me how she occasionally disciplined herself. When she went away from home, she would just listen. I decided to try it. I didn't even last for one evening. Even after I came home I still felt unnatural and as if I was in someone else's skin.

Now, I vow to practice listening again. This time I won't try such a drastic approach. It won't work anyway. I'll try watching the person who is talking. I'll listen so carefully that I won't have room to mentally plan my responses. I'll try very hard to respond by asking a question. I'll try to remind myself that our great and loving God is the master listener.

If I succeed with this listening idea, I'll probably have to write more just to get things off my back!

• • •

Eric left his baby and toddler years behind, but not his "Purple." As he grew, he still couldn't fall into dreamland without his fuzzy blue blanket. But he showed us he was a real boy who lovingly held pet frogs and toads. Their homes were always under overturned cardboard boxes. The homes were always very temporary though. Before long, there'd be a little boy searching for a lost pet.

Eric considered trapping mice for Mom a real adventure. I was delighted to be freed of the gruesome task. Once a mouse was caught, he'd parade trap and mouse around. He'd coax everyone to pet it, or at least feel its beautiful long tail.

Once after carrying out his catch he soon returned with big tears rolling down his cheeks. "Them there kittens eat my mouse," he sobbed.

The next time he knew what to do. He kept it safe in the garage. A few days later his Dad had an unpleasant task.

One day he squashed earthworms into "supper." It pleased him immensely that it was only Dad and him "that got two pockets." Mom and big sister "Lis" weren't that lucky.

I'm not familiar with these boyish antics. At home, we were girls. We always say the few boys we had around we turned into girls! But my mother could probably tell her share of stories about frogs, mice, toads, and worms.

• • •

As Alyssa grew, she worked to prove her independence. She gave up her blankie. She sat beside me with her notebook and pen and wrote her own *Connection* letters. She washed dishes, cleaned her own messes, and helped with the weekly cleaning. Only the snaps would remain unfastened after she dressed herself. She started making her bed each morning. "Don't you think I'm ready for school, Mom?" she would plead. She'd practice printing her name. The *A* was no problem ever since age three. But her *s*'s were backward and the *y* was impossible. One weekend, at a gathering, her older playmates had her trace her dotted name. I scolded myself in unbelief. Oh, teacher-mother! How could I forget that form of practice?

Baby Kyle went through a period where he just couldn't learn to crawl properly. At least not what I call proper. His method was convenient though. He found it possible to hold something in one hand and while sitting on the floor, move by paddling one foot forward very slowly. Now, you can't do that on your hands and knees. Maybe it's a smart way to get around! He thought it was, and it worked for a while!

• • •

When I was young and we'd go to the Albrecht grandparents' overnight, we always slept in their green toddler bed. At least, we slept there when we were small enough to fit in it.

Imagine my delight when that little bed was offered to any of their grandchildren. No one else wanted it and it was just what we needed. Eric was pushing Alyssa out of her crib.

Alyssa never had any use for a toddler bed. She skipped the small bed and went directly to the double spare bed. Now she has all the kicking, tossing, and turning space she needs.

I procrastinated about refinishing the bed. The paint looked thick and the job huge. But at the time, I knew Kyle's playpen would soon no longer work as a temporary crib. He needed Eric's beloved, white crib. Eric would get the toddler bed. It was time to tackle the thick coats of paint.

The old butcher knife didn't budge that tough, green paint. Nor did any of the other sharp objects I tried. It wasn't practical to use paint stripper with small children around. But I didn't want a green bed, either. In the end we sent it to brother-in-law Ken. He and his wife finally freed the bed of its green paint by disassembling it and power sanding each piece.

Now it glistens with its coat of dark walnut stain and varnish. We just had to find an odd-sized mattress, and it was ready for another century of nestling sleepy children.

I'm not so naive anymore. I know why my cousins and siblings had no use for that bed.

• • •

Rowdy just wasn't as rowdy as he used to be. When he ran, it was more of a hobble than a trot and it wasn't very fast anymore. The carriage was heavy for him and he wasn't strong enough to pull the garden scuffler. (Cultivator, my U.S. friend says you call it.) So every time we had a weedy garden we had to borrow a horse from the neighbors.

Now we only have pleasant youthful memories of Rowdy. And there's Mabel. She's big, black, gentle, and traffic-safe. She can even pull a scuffler. The children and I think she's perfect. Allan says we forgot to mention slow.

When we were horse shopping, Allan took the children to an auction. Eric got hooked. He loved to play auction sale. Alyssa wasn't interested in the game, so he had to wear many hats. First he was the announcer giving information like, "She's real wild, but kind of slow."

Next he was the whip boy who ran the horse while auction-ing it. Finally, out of breath, he'd sell the prize to his parents or siblings. Kyle ran beside with his own horse and his special chant, "La, la, la, la, la, la."

Our seasons of spring mud were rough on young Eric. He'd come in for a change of clothing, as his "eczema skin" couldn't handle being wet. When it bothered him he'd say, "The bees are stinging me, Mom." His heap of laundry was twice as high as his siblings'. When I pointed this out to his dad, he merely smiled and commented, "At least one boy's clean!"

One day while carrying him in for a nap, I rubbed one rough little foot and sympathized, "Aw, Eric, your poor little foot."

"It's okay, Mom," he cheered me. "I can still use it."

• • •

One of Allan's work friends had the privilege of doing mis-sion work in Africa one winter. We were delighted to journey with him through his numerous pictures.

It's another world. The grass huts, poverty, children drinking from cupped hands and eating with their fingers, and even the lack of variety in food. Elephants, hippos, giraffes, and monkeys thrilled the children.

The mission buildings surely must be considered mansions by the natives. As a homebody, I consider missionaries brave no matter the condition of the mission station. However, I couldn't help but compare them with David Livingstone, the doctor, explorer, and missionary in the land of Africa in the early 1800s. Malaria, jungle fever, wild animals, "Turks," and slave drivers were his constant enemies. Later, he was asked how he endured all those years of hardship, loneliness, and suffering while serving in Africa. He answered that it was because of a promise of the most sacred honor: "Lo, I am with you always, even unto the end of the world" (Matthew 28:20).

Year upon year has passed and Africa has changed more than David Livingston could have imagined possible. As Africa changed, the Western world changed at an even more rapid pace.

It's the promise that has not changed. Year upon year passes and always God stays the same: "Lo, I am with you always . . ."

• • •

If they need help with their clothes, my children will ask me to "off-button" them. They want their trailer "off-hooked," and say that Dad "off-hitched" the horse. When Eric has his big box of firewood carried up, he gleefully off-loads it into the woodbox.

The prefix *un-* doesn't have a spot in my children's vocabulary. I'm guessing they get the word *off* from our German dialect. Sometimes I'll correct them, but mostly I ignore it, hoping someday it'll correct itself. The day I found the word *off-load* in one of my favorite columnist's pieces was the day I gasped as I read: "An hour later I was off-loaded and ready to go."

I couldn't believe it. I read it again. Still it read *off-loaded*. To really top things, later he had written, "When the off-loading was done, she had an accurate count of plants."

"Listen to this," I told Allan. "Some big boy never learned to let go of his Dutchy phrases."

Later it struck me. Something was wrong. Never before had I detected a mistake in that columnist's articles, nor in any other part of that newspaper, for that matter. The dictionary would know, I knew.

Gulp! There it was with all the other common *off-* words like *off-season*, *offside*, and even *off-the-wall*. In bold, dark letters it read "off-load," and its meaning was simple: unload. Better get busy off-loading that wood, boys.

15

The Best Years

ONE MORNING I WAS LATE not because I pushed the snooze button (which is usually the reason I'm late). It was nothing in particular, just a host of little things that slowed me down. First the baby was hungry. While feeding him, I noticed Eric's wheezing was worse, so I dressed him and took him with us to the shop. Because we got out there late we came back in late. I had skipped packing lunches the night before in favor of going with the rest on neighborhood errands. So I was in the middle of packing lunch, frying eggs, and good-morning kisses when Allan's driver came. Whew! It wasn't a bad morning, but it did deserve a second cup of coffee. I suppose days filled with moments like that contribute to the deep weariness we feel at the end.

• • •

We call it the back room. It was intended to be used as a downstairs bedroom. We prefer to sleep next door to the tummy aches, nightmares, and thirsty throats, so our bedroom is upstairs beside the childrens'. That's why we have a back room. We have no other use for it besides holding the leftovers.

The children's dresser, extra chairs, car seats, and a bench found their way back there. Mostly, though, it's filled with toys. A table, chairs, and cupboards from my childhood and a child's desk from the neighbors. A barn from Allan's past, play animals, blocks, and tractors litter the floor. Dolls, dishes, papers, books, and baby toys add to the clutter.

I don't approve of a room like that. One day I decided that I didn't have to put up with it. So with three children in tow, I set out to transform that room.

We sorted toys. All the animals went into one ice cream bucket and the blocks in another. Up in the top cupboard they went. The dolls were neatly arranged in a crib. The toys that were only for clutter, not play, were packed in the upstairs closet. The bench went to the basement and the car seats to the spare room. Enough garbage to fill a shopping bag disappeared from the desk while Alyssa was busy sorting books. We rearranged the furniture and houseplants. The flip sofa, which we moved down from upstairs, gave the room a cozy feel.

The next morning, the children insisted I sit on the sofa in there with them while I wrote. They busily returned the room to its original state.

Eric would pass his days fixing puzzles. He was undaunted by our small selection. He'd fix one, put it away, and then start on the next. Over and over until his dad teased him that he could fix them in the dark!

Alyssa loved to make cards. For our project one winter month, we started with cookie cutter cards. If you trace around the cutters, you have pretty pictures to paste onto your card. We even recycled used gift tags by cutting them apart, then tracing our patterns on the sparkly paper. Next we cut pictures from magazines and made piles of cards.

• • •

Our children all enjoy talking. Maybe that's why we hear so many funny things.

Alyssa was stirring her hot chocolate with the end of her fork. "I'm just using the stem," she said. "I can't find my spoon."

Once she thought Eric should help her with her new set of paints. She searched in vain for another brush and was rather relieved when I found one for him. "But Mom," she cried in dismay. "This one has no whiskers."

Eric has a habit of doing everything but concentrating while we help him dress. One day, in frustration I asked, "Eric, are you a rag doll?"

"Nope," he answered too cheerfully. "A rag boy."

There. Now you have a glimpse of why life with children is never boring. We learn to see things from a different viewpoint.

• • •

If there's such a thing as a sixteen-month-old bookworm, then Kyle was one from an early age. He was even addicted to certain types of books. They were the ones full of animal pictures. He would sit on the floor paging back and forth, back and forth, cooing softly to his animal friends. The other children knew to wait until he was napping before they brought out their favorite stories. Otherwise they knew they'd be interrupted by animal stories.

If he wasn't selling them by auction, Eric loved to put animals—no matter what form—in a cage. Imagine his delight when

Aunt Kathryn gave him a small wire cage with two chocolate rabbits in it! His voice reached a high-pitched squeak as he imagined what could be put in it. Chicks, guinea pigs, bunnies . . .

And Alyssa. She soon discovered that she could squeeze beside me for some quiet moments on the recliner while the boys slept. Only, the moments weren't that quiet. It wasn't long before she'd start her wishing. Once she brought along a new spring Sears catalog with its beautiful playground sets. The coveted one had a slide with water squirting down it. Just perfect for warm summer days, she thought.

Next, new shoes for Alyssa were high on the need list. Her old ones had grown terribly old, she loudly informed me. Why, there was even a little spot on the toe that was peeling. But new shoes were quickly forgotten after a town lady walked past with her dog. "Oh, Mom," she sighed, "you should buy me a female puppy 'cause female puppies never run away like Georgie did. Then I would get a leash and take her for a walk every day." With that she added the usual "Oh, that would be so much fun!"

No amount of explaining—how to be thankful for what we have and that more doesn't mean happiness—would stop her wishing. Even talking about all the children with much less didn't bother her for more than a few minutes. In frustration I said, "Alyssa, you need to get red wings." Then I told her of the little bunny who was always wishing too. He gleefully jumped at the chance to use the wishing pond old Mr. Groundhog told him of. When he got there, a beautiful bird with red wings flew away. What did he wish for but red wings—just like the bird. Of course, red wings are perfect for red birds but never for bunnies, and he spent a miserable night. Next morning he had no choice but to go and wish them off again.

Not a very logical story, but she soaked it up! Now when she starts with "I wish I had . . ." we laugh and quickly finish with "red wings"!

• • •

When I woke to the pitter-patter of raindrops, I joyfully rehearsed my mental list of rainy day jobs. It's a funny list—things I never find time to squeeze in between the mowing, gardening, and weed eating. I had promised myself that when it rained again I'd file the bookwork, take care of the phone calls, carry garbage from the basement, put the books back on the spare bedroom's bookshelf (the baby had fun one day), unpack some cases of shoes in the store, buy a wedding gift, and write. But the day didn't exactly go as planned.

"If I'd cry about everything I lose or break, I'd be sad indeed," my sister once stated. Add "spill" and I know exactly what she's saying. On that rainy morning while I was adding a piece of wood to the fire, I accidentally shoved my teakettle off the stove, which in turn sent the coffeepot, complete with filter and coffee grounds, crashing to the floor.

Eric quietly watched me clean the soupy, grainy mess before advising, "If I were a big 'women' I would be very careful and I would put my coffeepot at the other end of the stove."

Yes, yes, little boy with the big advice. You would be careful because you are lucky enough to be like your dad. Alyssa didn't fare so well, but usually those losses, breaks, and spills can be quickly compensated, and we move on.

My glasses are a different story. I'm always going, where are they? Where could they be? How can you lose something that should be on your head? But I did and do. Sometimes I just go without for a while. Partly to teach myself a lesson, partly because I'm still hoping to find them, and partly because I can get along without them when I'm not sewing or doing extra reading.

. . .

On another morning, I wondered how I'd managed to so efficiently set up the makings of a bad day. Actually, it started the night before. We were at Doddys', so we didn't go to bed until late.

That next morning the alarm clock failed to rouse me, so Allan had to eat cold cereal while I hastily packed his lunch. Eric decided it was a good morning to rise with the sun, and woke up everyone else in the process. So then I had three grumpy, tired children. There was the lukewarm coffee I just couldn't get to. Plus, I had not gotten a head start on work left over from yesterday—which was already enough work to keep a woman busy for a day. One without children. Through my foggy mind filtered a new poem I read recently by A. W., a fellow mother, who gave me permission to use it here.

> The whirlwind of the day is dead; I make a round from bed to bed.
> I tuck a blanket, stroke a cheek, and note a dried and salty streak.
> September duties of the day, so deafening and immense,
> With haste, this moment, shrivel into insignificance.
> Demanding corn and pining pears, the chili recipe's cold stares,

How could it be? How could it be? These shouters got the
    best of me.
And our dear children merely got the rest of me—my
    worst;
A growl, some rage, impatient sighs, an aggravation burst?

The whirlwind of the day is dead; I wipe a tear and hang
    my head.
Had I but giv'n these my best; to chili, pears, and corn, the
    rest.
Forgive me, Lord. And if the sun tomorrow climbs and sets,
I pray that by your grace, there'll be no ten o'clock regrets.
                                   ("Ten O'clock Regrets")

Then you can only pray for patience and love. You realize
that on days like this it's not the work that gets done that matters. It's that which you graciously left undone.

• • •

There seemed nothing to do that morning but squabble
about toys they had played with for too many months. I sat at
the sewing machine, thinking dark thoughts and peddling fu-
riously through the fussing. Suddenly, I stood up. "Enough of
this," I announced. "Let's go outside."

Then the whining began. It was too cold. The sun wasn't
shining. Weren't they just outside yesterday?

I pulled coats, caps, and boots on through the grumbling.
Eventually we tumbled outside to find the sun shining after all.

Returning borrowed items to the neighbors was a joy in the
bright sunshine. The snowbanks were still white and high, and

the wind chilly; but the sun shone smiling and warm. Everyone begged to walk to the river. From there they spied a bare patch in our meadow.

"Let's have a picnic lunch, Mom," someone suggested. "It's big enough for us all to sit on."

Now it was my turn to declare it too cold. At the disappointed faces, I quickly added that maybe they could eat on the porch.

That set the race to the playhouse to pull out the little lawn chairs while I warmed lunch. I opted to sit inside the door where it was warm. Kyle had difficulty eating with his puffy mittens, and it was too cold to take them off. Finally he pushed through the door for me to feed him each bite. He quickly relaxed in his porch seat to chew. When the plates were empty, the children trooped in glowing, with the words "Dinner was so good. It's so nice out there."

My brave girlie added, "It's so warm; let's go out and collect twigs."

The sewing machine hummed in the quiet house while they filled their pails with twigs.

Eric returned to announce a patch of bare lawn, "Just in case you wanted to mow lawn in the middle of the winter."

Now I see it. These are the best years.

16

The (Third) New Baby

WHEN OUR THIRD CHILD came along, he was a charmer and quickly became the center of our domain. We named him Kyle Allan, weighing a healthy six pounds twelve ounces. The first week he gained another pound; the second week, still another. Early on I hoped he'd slow down before he ate us out of house and home.

In the beginning, two-year-old Eric simply tolerated the newcomer's presence. For him, life continued as usual. There were "farms" to build and a dog to teach how to catch a ball. Eric also kept "Purple" to cuddle whenever life got tough. Alyssa took her new mothering duties much more seriously. She did find out that it was okay to venture outside, once she determined that the baby was here for keeps.

I rapidly ate my own baby-raising words again. I always said I would not give another one of my babies a soother (or a lolly, pacifier, nippy, or whatever you call it). But when the baby's little forehead wrinkled and he beat the air with his tiny fists and wiggled and squirmed because his tummy hurt, then in we popped a round, blue soother. It satisfied his sucking needs and provided the comfort he needed to help him sleep.

He also was allowed to sleep in his car seat stored in the house. I wasn't going to let that happen again either. Then one night, after leaving the comfort and warmth of my bed every hour, I had enough. The next night he slept in his car seat and only got me up once!

We all have those days when we hope that tomorrow will be a better one. I remember one day when it rained all day. The dinner dishes got washed at 4:00 p.m. and the floor swept just before suppertime. Supper was pleasant enough: pancakes, sausage, apple wedges, and hot chocolate, perfect for a chilly evening. Normally, I try to serve a full-course evening meal after Allan works out in the cold all day with only lunch-box fare.

Whenever I have an "old woman who lived in a shoe" day, I try to remember the "Old Woman in the Shoe" from Alyssa's Precious Moments book; instead of succumbing to frustration, the woman "asked God to help her and show his great love, by blessing her house with his help from above."

In the children's book, the old woman looks so sweet kneeling there by her shoe full of children.

"It looks so simple," my sister commented.

It is that simple. Isn't it? We just forget.

• • •

Alyssa is thrilled we now have a big family just as our neighbors do. During Kyle's first days she often expressed her thrill with, "Oh, Mom, now we have lots of children like Dougs' and Reubens.'" (And that was before the fourth one came along.) I well remember the first time I herded all three of our children into church, which was a little overwhelming. I managed only because of kind hands.

We all enjoyed the new little one, a picture of health with chubby cheeks, coos, and smiles. My joy made me think of a line from Amish author David Kline: "While we were blessed in getting rain, there are regions that are not so fortunate and suffered lost production. For that reason we don't want to be too euphoric."

Along those lines we humbly say, "While we are blessed with a healthy baby, there are many with empty arms or sick babies. For this reason we don't want to be too euphoric."

• • •

My sister says her friend wrote and said she finished her sewing and now she's making cards. Whew! Hats off to women who work in such an organized manner. The Mommy Over There does. I guess I learned my work habits from the Mommy Far Away. If I made cards, then I would probably write that I made a few cards that afternoon and sewed a little. I only get a little here and a little there done each day. I'm not sure if you ever get done that way.

Alyssa is the one who labeled the mommies, by the way. The Mommy Far Away is only a mile and a half down the road. I suppose that's far away to a little mind, whose Mommy Over There is only on the other side of the door.

We sometimes pick up new insights about our children through careful listening. One day a visitor came with a gift for new baby Kyle, toy animals for Eric, and a coloring book and crayons for Alyssa. Alyssa and the visitor sat down together to color a picture. That's when Alyssa dropped the bomb: "I can't color."

"Oh, yes you can," our visitor insisted.

"No, I just scribble," was the prompt reply.

"Oh, but I did too when I was three," came our friend's answer. Only after a lot of coaxing did Alyssa reluctantly pick up her crayon.

Encouraging words like "great job" and "that looks good" from my friend soon had Alyssa confidently coloring her page.

Her watching mother knew exactly why Alyssa was sure that she couldn't color. My standards were too high for her abilities. I would outline her picture and instruct her not to go over those lines. After all, I wanted my little girl to know how to properly color when she went to school.

All I got was a girl who thought she couldn't color.

Now, the lesson I took from that incident is not to stop teaching my daughter how to color neatly. It is that I must not smother her. You know, smother her eagerness, her enjoyment, her creativeness.

• • •

When I bemoan my meager accomplishments while tending to little ones, too often I compare my days to when I was a teacher. Those days, I knew at the end of the day what all was accomplished. It was there before me in the stacks of workbooks. Then I'd leave for home, content with a scene of checked books and lessons prepared for the new day.

Young mothers just don't have it like that. At the end of the day you gaze at your kitchen. The tablecloth hangs crooked, the windows are smeared, and visitors would assume that the floor never saw a broom that day. But best of all is what's in the midst of all this: chubby-faced, pajama-clad children. Waiting with their blankies to say prayers and get their good-night kisses. Then it's worth it all.

• • •

An outdoor outing with three started off in grand style with the baby in his stroller, Eric on his hobbyhorse, and Alyssa pushing her own stroller and baby. The return trip was much smoother with everyone, and their gear, piled up on the baby's stroller. I got every penny out of the money I paid for that stroller!

I was still contentedly changing double diapers when Eric decided to take potty training into his own hands. One day his dad brought home a bag of pink bubble gum as a reward. Then there was gum everywhere! The table, chairs, floor, bed frames, and—once—on baby dear! But I didn't mind it if it meant quicker potty training. Alyssa's lessons were a horror, and the pessimists told me boys were worse. Whew!

As Kyle grew to a fat, contented three-month-old, he no longer needed a car seat to sleep in, and rarely a soother. At last I felt like I could be the mother I *meant* to be the third time around.

With three children, we graduated to a carriage. Now Dad, Mom, and baby have the open front seat all to themselves. The older ones are cozy and content in their back covered seat with the clear storm front. They love it, and so do I. Now when we go away without Dad they sing and talk in the back, and I drive. With the buggy, someone or something, like the blankets, was always sliding off the seat—always some kind of distraction to take my focus off my driving.

The little details. Even those are wonderfully taken care of. Like very busy moms. We need to rest too, but sometimes we're too busy, we think. No matter. The baby needs to be fed.

Ah, just what we need. A chance to put up our feet without even a twinge of guilt. Baby is hungry and needs to be fed. The Scriptures remind us that our Father planned it all.

• • •

Baby brother is still chubby and contented, but he's attracted to his siblings' play and longs to join in. Mother says, baby dear, rest in my arms just a little longer. It makes me think of lines from Alfred, Lord Tennyson's "What Does Little Birdie Say?"

What does little birdie say,
In her nest at peep of day?
"Let me fly," says little birdie.
"Mother, let me fly away."
"Birdie, rest a little longer,
Till the little wings are stronger."
So she rests a little longer,
Then she flies away.

What does little baby say,
In her bed at peep of day?
Baby says, like little birdie,
"Let me rise and fly away."
"Baby sleep a little longer,
Till the little limbs are stronger."
If she sleeps a little longer,
Baby, too, shall fly away.

• • •

One summer day I reflected that while there was much we didn't get done, we had all worked hard at work worth doing. There was sweet corn in jars and wood in the basement. Allan was at home, so that made it a good day before I even crawled out of bed. Everything is easier with Daddy around. Discipline for the selfish daughter is as simple as "Next time, you'll share with your brother." And the rope used for playing horse is hung out of reach. Eric's owies from his fall off a trike are swiftly forgotten when "Ambulance Daddy" comes over with his siren wailing full blast. No wonder they're always asking for Dad. Mom's *so boring.*

Of all the things that could wait until next week, the peaches could not. Besides, I was dreadfully hungry for fresh peach pie. So I quickly set my bake oven on top of the Coleman camp stove to heat. I rolled out a piecrust from the freezer and brushed it with beaten egg. I sliced the peaches at high speed and mixed them with sugar and Perma-Flo and a dash of cinnamon. I made the topping with flour, brown sugar, and real butter. Ah, delicious!

Oops! All the while I was concocting my pie while heating the bake oven, I was baking a plastic dish—the unlucky remnant from one of the children's baking sprees.

I was determined that my pie be baked; time was fleeing and my options were few: fire up my woodstove or clean my bake-oven camp stove. So I moved everything to the lawn and got busy cleaning. Finally I could bake pie on the lawn. Probably contaminated pie, but at least I wasn't burning Tupperware.

• • •

Oh, they're all so different. Our children that is. The ladies at church say it. I've heard it from strangers on the street and from close friends too. I always nod in agreement. "But not that different," I mentally add.

Our two oldest are pipsqueaks who eat like sparrows. Nothing unusual for either of our families. We soon learned a cracker at 11:00 a.m. would spoil lunch. Food tasted better if your spoon was an airplane. We also learned the "no dessert till the plate is empty" rule had to be firmly enforced.

They like to read books, write, and color. Talking and playing pretend games are high on the list of favorites. Eric inherited more of his dad's easygoing nature than his big sister did, but then again, even twins aren't exactly alike.

Kyle showed us the meaning of different. No crawling for him, just scooting on his bottom. He didn't even attempt to walk until fifteen and a half months old! Easygoing just doesn't describe him.

His real love is the outdoors. It's never too cold or wet for him. We could never come inside without him sobbing with disappointment. The most remarkable difference is at mealtime. He scoops up his porridge, then begs for an egg. He sighs with satisfaction and drinks his milk. He doesn't know what spoon airplanes are, and he always gets dessert.

Oh, they're all quite different!

17

The Joys of Home

FUNNY HOW CERTAIN INCIDENTS bring flashbacks from the past. Like when I dressed my little ones for winter outdoor fun when they were too young to help much. We pulled on vests, then coats, and hook-and-eyed each one. There were three sets of mittens for three sets of hands. A kerchief or cap to protect each little head. Then we wrapped a long scarf on top of it all. Last of all we'd find warm boots for everyone. I never finished this dressing ritual without the urge to glance out the window and sigh, "The snow has melted."

The line comes from a poem my classmate recited at a Christmas program. It opened with, "By the time Junior is suited, and capped and booted . . ."

The rest of the poem eludes my memory, save for its memorable ending: "the snow has melted."

• • •

My aunt wrote that they were very busy stripping wallpaper, mudding cracks, and painting the house they just moved into. She ended with, "Someday we'll probably look back and say we enjoyed that too."

I know she will. Someday when enough time has elapsed to forget the disaster, the backache, the sore shoulders, and the paint-splattered spectacles. That is when she'll say, "That was actually kind of fun."

Just like us young mothers. We're constantly hearing, "These are your best years. Enjoy your children when they are young." Most days we can agree. There are other days though. Days when everyone gets up at 5:00 a.m., the two-year-old refuses to nap, and you haven't seen anything besides the four walls of your home for days on end. Those days we grit our teeth, try to smile, and dream of better years ahead. Someday, though, we'll look back and all we'll remember are the freshly bathed, sleepy-eyed babies lisping their prayers. Then we'll sigh and say, "Oh, those were the best years."

• • •

We were away for a few days. We had excellent company and food. The cottage was probably nicer than our house, besides being situated in front of a lake. There was a boat in the lake, with fish to catch. No work interrupted the attention our children desired. Just perfect.

But one morning back at home a few days later, Eric woke up. He laughed and laughed. A pure, delighted, bubbling laugh. "Eric, what's so funny?" I asked. I was answered with more laughter. I knew then that there was nothing funny. It was joy. The joy of coming home.

• • •

Her name is Lizzie and she's five years old. She likes to pick dandelions and blow their fuzzy tops. She wishes to do jobs much too big for her, like milking a cow and making supper. When preschool days were over she sat and pouted on the porch. She even kicked the top step until Mother came. We all shivered when she climbed the silo and walked along the barn roof.

She's so real, the Lizzie in our bedtime storybook.

Bless the writers who write for our little "Lizzies." Surely they don't get much recognition. Five-year-olds are too busy thinking about the character and cannot stretch their brains to include the author. At Christmastime we gave Alyssa her copy of the first of Mrs. Gid's "Lizzie" books. Once again she'll be impressed with Lizzie, and I with the excellent play of words.

One morning I wrote: "I'm mother to three little children and a tiny guinea fowl chick. Right now I'm failing them all. I can't get my day off the ground."

Their dad got up to leave for work early, as usual. The children were not sleeping as usual though, but were wide awake and checking on their chick. When Dad's driver came, they begged to show him the new pet. Dad glanced desperately about before shrugging and asking, "In a dirty house like this?"

"Messy," I corrected tartly.

How do you convince a guinea fowl chick to eat and drink? Especially when all you want to do is crawl back in bed for a nap? Or better yet, drink coffee and read.

I tried everything. I put its food on shiny tinfoil. It wasn't curious. Next we tried a thin gruel and dipped its head. Still couldn't whet its appetite. Finally I used a medicine dropper and force-fed it. My daughter howled that it was going to die. The baby copied her, but only because he had ended his night too early. After the feeding I was sure we'd all soon be joining the howls. The bird lay in a pathetic heap gasping for its last breaths, I was sure. I closed the lid on the pathetic scene and set everything on top of the stove shelf.

Baby soon looked sweet with his eyes closed and wrapped in a cozy blanket in his crib. The chick had revived while I was rocking the baby. Soon the chick was peeping and running again.

Eric picked up his animals and wood pieces. I quickly braided Alyssa's hair before she cleared the breakfast table. The sun rose. Maybe I could be a mother to three little ones *and* a guinea fowl after all.

It wasn't to be though, despite our best efforts. Ah, it's good to be a mother to just human little ones.

Eventually children do grow big enough to do the jobs they coveted. Sometimes they're even as fun as they imagined. I remember when Alyssa first started to get the mail in. First she'd wait until baby Kyle was napping. She'd take the footstool, then look carefully for traffic before marching across the road to step up and fetch the treasures the mailman brought.

"Did he bring the *Cection*?" Eric would ask anxiously, referring to *Connection* magazine.

At the shake of her head, he would accuse me. "Mom, did you not write a story? They don't give us a *Cection*."

• • •

When we went away that cold, stormy day, everyone was feeling fine. No colds, coughs, or stomachaches in sight. When it was time to bundle everyone to go home, the baby prattled in a croaky voice and had a deep, whoopy cough that ended with a bark. Strange, I thought, but he was acting fine so I ignored it.

That night we heard more of those whoops and barks and occasionally he struggled for air. "Just like Eric," I sighed.

"Asthma." One minute you're fine, the next you're struggling for breath. I quickly applied Eric's puffer. I knew I shouldn't, but it was dark and I had to do something for my struggling baby. The deep cough was very strange. Eric always had weak, tickly coughs. Nothing deep that barked the way the baby's did. "All cases must be different," I surmised. "After all, what else comes and goes as quickly as asthma?"

The next morning he was much better except for the bark, which didn't seem to bother him. So we all left to go to my parents'. Everyone had a good day until its end, when Kyle started another attack. He couldn't get enough air and coughed with each breath. I applied the puffer and held him beside an open door for fresh air. By the time the driver arrived to take him to the emergency room he was doing better.

At the sight of the nurses he started to cry, which set him to whooping and barking. "Mmm," they murmured, nodding their heads. I confessed my puffer sharing and they kindly reassured me that it was okay.

"The nurses say your baby has the croup," the doctor announced. His arrival set off Kyle's crying and whooping and barking.

"Hear that bark, ma'am? That's croup. Puffers don't help croup. It restricts the airways in the throat, whereas asthma is in the lungs. Cold or damp air relieves croup, not a ventilator."

They treated my baby for croup and armed me with plenty of information. I vowed to let my doctors diagnose my children's illnesses in the future.

• • •

Our eight chickens protested the cold by only laying two eggs a day. That was before I read a suggestion in *Farming Magazine*. Mix warm water with their feed. So we carried hot water to the chickens. By the time we had it mixed with the laying mash, it was warm and the chickens devoured it. No one eats at the feeding trough anymore. They strut and peck at the chaff on the floor until their bowl of warm mash comes. Then there's a mad dash and a furious pecking until it's gone. After a few weeks of this treat, we collected six to seven eggs daily, sometimes even eight.

• • •

It was blowing snow and cold as usual the day the children decided to eat lunch at the picnic table. Eager for change, I slapped ham, lettuce, and mustard between bread slices. We packed carrot sticks and tarts and mixed hot chocolate. Everyone carried a piece of lunch as we bucked the drifts to the shop. There we arranged our lunch on the picnic table.

While eating our sandwiches in the warm, bright shop, Eric smiled cheerfully. "Oh, I feel like I could laugh!" he said. Just what we needed.

• • •

The Waterloo (Ont.) region is not a good place for women to live, the daily newspaper announced. What could be wrong with living in that high-tech, successful area? I wondered. Too much stress, a study finds. More than one in three women living there say they have high levels of stress.

For a lot of women, money, money, money is the big stress. Then there's workplace stress. Added to that is the stress of finding sitters for children and dropping them off and picking them up. Plus, there's the children's schedule to set up and follow.

A woman interviewed by the paper said that women have more stress in life because they want to do everything perfectly, or close to it. Amanda Weber, a stress management teacher, told the *Record* that "women need to find a way to manage their stress because stress is a reality that isn't likely to go away in our 'always on' culture" (*Waterloo Region Record*, April 25, 2014).

We live beside this stressed-out region. Thankfully, most of the women's stress factors are not mine. I am not the provider; I do not have a job away from home, nor do I plan a schedule for my children. But some of their stress seems to have filtered over. That urge to be perfect seems to hit every culture in first-world countries.

We want well-behaved children with clean, neat clothes. Our gardens are hoed, lawns are mowed, and homes are scrubbed well, while our children are peppered with, "What would people think if they saw this mess?" Mother is in a tizzy because company is coming and they must not see lack of management.

We compare ourselves to the women beside us. Finding ourselves lacking, we rev our engines into overtime, with a stress load to match. The "always on the go" culture seeps through too. In the midst of our comings and goings, we forget to be happy, contented keepers at home.

Anna Quindlen writes in her book *Loud and Clear*, "I wish I had treasured the doing a little more and the getting it done a little less." That should take care of stress! To thoroughly enjoy your hands in the warm water and soap, and the sparkle of each clean dish, instead of just swishing them through the water before rushing to the next job. Each red berry would be a treasure found, rather than being one step nearer the row's end. We would pause to admire and enjoy our clean room instead of rushing to clean the next one.

This is easier to do after your baby reaches two and a half years, I found. No more races to finish a job while the baby naps.

The worst stress is that which you create yourself. Like my bad habit of waiting until the last minute to get ready to go away. This might have worked reasonably well when I was on my own, but not anymore! Before going shopping with Aunt Laura one day, I hoed in the garden as long as I dared. Tension was high as I rushed around, barking orders, scrubbing babies, and yanking on clean clothes.

"Mom," Alyssa tried, "every time you talk, you sound really grumpy."

"I know," came my quick reply. "But if I didn't, we wouldn't be ready on time."

Later, while waiting on the porch swing for the driver, I realized my mistake. "I'm sorry, Alyssa. I wouldn't have had to talk grumpy to be ready on time," I apologized.

She sighed. "Now we could still be slowly getting ready instead of waiting and waiting," she lamented.

I didn't bother mentioning that the driver was half an hour late.

But each day brings stress we didn't create and perhaps cannot avoid. It does not have to burn us, though. Spend a little time each day to talk with our Creator, who is capable of carrying the heaviest stress loads. Read and study the Lord's words and meditate on his teachings. Gather "daily manna."

Sing joyfully while you work. Thank God for the blessings of a family and church who will help with the stress of financial and work overload if necessary.

18

All in a Day's Work

As A CHILD, when September neared, I always anticipated it coming to set me free. Free of the bushels of corn, cucumbers, peaches, tomatoes, lawn mowing, and potato bug picking. Free to return to the wonderful world of books.

Now, as a mother, September just brings more corn, peaches, cucumbers, tomatoes, and no freedom. Nor would I want any. I delight in putting away summer's bounty for my family.

September no longer changes much for us. Just children on their scooters flashing by morning and evening. But as Alyssa's first opportunity approached when she'd join others for her very first taste of structured learning, I knew things were changing. When anyone just mentioned kindergarten, you could see her delight!

At the time, Alyssa frequently reminded me she'd be five on her next birthday. Did I know that some people go to school when they are five? She had other discoveries: when it's your birthday, you don't help sing the happy birthday song. She gave a forewarning to Eric. He may not sing when it's his birthday. She also shared her wisdom with Uncle Jody. She then watched carefully all through his happy birthday song to see if he understood. We'll see if she remains silent when we sing for her!

It's not uncommon to wish to do things we can't. Like type. I wish I could type my own *Connection* letters. That would relieve someone of the job of typing each of my handwritten letters. As usual though, my eyes were opened. I learned to be thankful for what I have. Very thankful. Knowing how to write cursively is faster than printing for most of us. Better than knowing how to type, I learned.

Our local newspaper ran a story of a twelve-year-old boy who cannot write cursively. No fault of his own. Cursive writing is no longer deemed a necessary part of the public school system. The boy in the article was fortunate, as his father stepped into the picture. Their summer holiday's goal was to learn the art. "I guess I'll need it to sign my name a few times," was the boy's remark.

Oh my. That started my teacher blood boiling. It reminded me of the required fifteen minutes of cursive writing practice we had three times a week. I doubt it was anyone's favorite class and I'm sure no one valued it properly. There are so many rules to remember. You have to sit properly, hold your pencil correctly, and slant your paper, with a liner underneath, just so. The liner helps slant the letters correctly and gives them straight backs. It matters how high your letters are and how they are spaced.

So many rules to remember and yet you must stay relaxed enough for the writing to flow smoothly. No wonder writing class was often closed with a sigh. Hearing of that twelve-year-old and thinking of the many students like him make all the sighs, correcting, and checking page after page of practice work worth it. I'm confident all my former students can write cursively, and I know some can write it well.

Did you ever have the privilege of reading the writing of someone who learned the art with a fountain pen? Our teacher's guide for cursive writing is from that era. Now let me see you write *that* well. Keep writing!

• • •

There was no excuse anymore to not go out and do the cutting for the next day's shop work. I wished there were, so I let a few more days slip by, hoping something might turn up. It didn't. I had taken a break after Kyle was born. When he turned two, I no longer had the "baby" excuse. I took my three little ones along to play while I cut.

I'm not particularly fond of the job and it takes a lot of my time. Not the cutting, but the helping to set up a horsie game, unloosening a little foot, or fixing the tractor crashes. With all the interruptions the cutting isn't even boring. You're just glad when you have a chance to actually cut.

We would then take the long way back to the house after I finished. There were horses to see, chickens to feed and eggs to collect, and cats and kittens to pet. By the time we reached the house, it was likely to be lunchtime or close enough to it.

"Our days just fly by," Alyssa commented on one such day, before she went to school. I heartily agreed and wondered about the merits of doing the cutting.

As winter deepens, our shop work varies. We don't always have to do cutting. That's when I notice some of the benefits of our daily shop time. Long days inside just aren't as intriguing for the little ones, which results in more squabbles to settle and more Mom attention. On the days we do the cutting, Dad doesn't have to, so everyone gets a little more daddy time. That gives me a little more quiet time to get done what I didn't do in the morning.

Sometimes I'm just a little slow at appreciating the good things in life!

• • •

I always felt bad that our guests had to sleep surrounded by camouflage, turkey decoys, and other hunting paraphernalia. "If I had a closet, I'd clean the spare room," Allan always replied whenever I fussed about it.

When the piles increased, I finally decided if a closet was what he needed, I'd make him one. Having zero carpentry skills left me with few options. There would be no hammer or nails involved in this project.

I found two big bags and yanked open the door of the existing spare room closet. Once the closet was empty, one bag was filled with junk, the other held thrift store donations, and the items in the small pile on the floor found new homes in other closets.

After the closet was refilled with hunting gear, my daughter waltzed into the clean, sunny room.

"What a beautiful, clean room!" she cried.

I'm sure my guests will breathe a silent agreement.

• • •

When Eric was still taking naps, he arranged everything just so. A row of books was set neatly against the wall; a stack of books was piled beside his pillow. A pile of Kleenex had to be in one corner and his favorite blanket on his pillow. Finally he was ready to snuggle under the covers.

When baby brother observed this naptime ritual, he decided to forgo the beloved rocking chair. That is, if he could arrange his crib to look like Eric's bed. So we propped books along the side and set one by his pillow. After his favorite blankie was in place, he happily snuggled under his covers, just like a big boy.

I miss the rocking, but relish the extra reading and writing time.

Long winter evenings meant reading stories from the children's big books. Stories from Benji or Lizzie or Laura Ingalls Wilder thrilled everyone but Kyle as a baby. There were not enough pictures and the pages moved too slowly. We learned to have a stack of picture books on hand that he could page through while we enjoyed our story.

One evening after we had settled with a timeless Benji book, I announced the title, *Time for a Haircut.*

Eric wrinkled his nose, gave a little shiver and shrank further into his seat. "No," he violently shook his head. "I don't want a—" He stopped short and laughed with the rest of us.

"Is it Benjie's turn?" he sheepishly asked.

• • •

At school we once recited a poem that began, "The hardest thing on a farm, I think, is how to teach a calf to drink."

Maybe. But have you ever tried to teach three young children to herd a flock of fowl? Right after our breakfast, we let the birds out of their cramped pen in the barn and into fresh pasture. There was fresh food and water just inside the open gate, and if we walked slowly enough, the birds would walk right in. "Remember, walk very slowly," I cautioned as Eric ran to open the door.

Eagerly the chickens came running and flapping from their nightly shelter. They settled down to enjoy their walk, pecking and scratching as they went. We were there to head them in the right direction and keep them moving.

One morning, I exhaled in relief when I saw the first bird walking to the waiting food dish. Just like that, a fat fryer strayed after a bug, and Alyssa dashed to bring him back. Eric quickly dove to catch one of his beloved baby turkeys. Kyle, not to be outdone, toddled to the middle of the flock, crying, "Shoo! Shoo! Shoo!"

Like an overflowing river, the birds streamed in many directions. Eric and Alyssa scattered the small groups in their haste to round them up. Each returned happily carrying a captured bird. The count was two birds for our pen. But Eric enjoyed the chase too much. He quickly set his turkey down, and away it ran again. One bird for our pen.

All around the pasture, small groups of birds were straining at the fence, trying to reach the lone bird at the feeding trough. Slowly, we chased them around to the open doorway. At the last minute, Kyle ran to guard the gateway and the birds ran back to their original spots. After much shooing, coaxing, and even catching the last ones, we finally had the flock behind the fence. Relieved, I turned to fill the water fountains. I spun quickly to Alyssa's screeches: "Mom, Mom, the chickens are out!"

I stared stupidly at the open gate, and at Eric, who had just returned with his recaptured turkey. He was carefully guiding it to the food and water bowls while the rest of the flock abandoned all for wide-open spaces.

The hardest thing on a farm, I think . . .

• • •

On a day when I devoured an envelope of material written by a writer friend, I felt like I'd had a day of vacation. No, not quite. I'd better say an hour of vacation, lest I stir jealousy!

Nothing about the beginning of the day hinted that it would feel like a vacation day. It was the end of winter and the sun refused to shine, so all signs pointed in the opposite direction.

The children were up before I started any of my early morning chores. Up and whining for a story, for breakfast, and for whatever else their tired little minds could think to whine about. That's why the two boys and I were rocking and singing when Alyssa left for school, instead of doing morning work. Which in turn was why my morning was half spent before my helper at the store, Johanna, and I reached the stack of boxes full of shoes waiting to be shelved. "A good morning should do it," I had told her earlier.

But as I said before, this wasn't exactly my version of a good morning. Especially when the boys continued their bickering and lunchtime was here before we had made more than a dent in the stack of boxes.

While I made lunch, the boys were impressed with Johanna's puzzle-finding skills, and I with her patience. Eventually, we wound down to naptime, which Kyle stoutly declared he didn't need. Not in the mood for a scene, I headed for the stairs, proclaiming myself in dire need of one. Eric, who didn't nap anymore, decided he needed one too. To aggravate his brother, I figured. Then Kyle whined, "But who will stay with me?"

We remedied that situation by adjusting the stairway door to stay open while he played and we slept. We were barely curled under our mink blankets when I heard a pitter-patter on the stairs. I was careful to keep my eyes closed as he nestled beside me. Dull days, early risings, and stressful mornings bring sweet rest. When I awoke later, my youngest slumbered on. I even changed my mind about Eric trying to be aggravating when I saw him curled up in his little bed, breathing deeply. A house this unusually quiet deserves something special, I decided.

I found it in the mailbox. A stack of delightful writing from a correspondent plus a favorite magazine. That's how I knew it was vacation day. Such a day I must guard carefully, for it usually comes my way unexpectedly only about once a year. I needed to seize the moment, let everything go, and make the most of its stay. The only preparation required was a cup of coffee, my stack of mail, and the recliner. I let the hour slip blissfully by between sips of black liquid and reading of hosting a Shia Muslim exchange student, events surrounding the death of the king of Saudi Arabia, and the small details of a trip to Vancouver Island to attend a brother's wedding. Mamas just returned from vacation are happy, relaxed mamas. Especially if their children had long naps.

Starting in the back room and sweeping my way around the house kept their dad from knowing that Mama had been vacationing. Unless he was suspicious of her good mood. "Luxury need not have a price; comfort itself is a luxury," wrote Geoffrey Beene.

• • •

I too began baking on my own around age seven. In that bliss, I never noticed my mother practicing her patience, nor the smeared cupboard doors and cookbooks. They must have been the same as in my own kitchen, now, along with the familiar greasy hands, shiny dress, and just-scraped bowls clinging with too much dough. The trail of spills, messes, and breakage Alyssa leaves behind resemble my own when I was seven. Or maybe *still*, according to my husband's honey-do list and the trash can.

Unlike Alyssa, I did not have the misfortune of being followed by a younger brother with a light touch and systematic brain. One day Eric noticed that the encyclopedia set was not in the correct order. Even though it's stored in the second-highest shelf, Eric didn't consider it too much of a problem to fix it. Up the high chair and onto the third shelf he went. Standing on tiptoe, he carefully removed one of the offending books and climbed back down before setting the book on the floor. One climb. Two climbs. Three climbs. The fourth climb was necessary to shove the remaining books in order. At last he was ready to haul the books back up. One at a time, until at last he could say with satisfaction, "They are now all in the right order."

19

One Thousand Beautiful Things

SHE SITS AND WAITS a mere two feet from where a railroad bridge used to span the river and road far below. Cold breezes whistle over her flattened neck and ruffle her feathers. A blizzard swirls several inches of snow around her. Still she sits, patiently protecting what is hers.

Men climb the hill where the train used to chug up. Once, they chased her off with sticks and stole two of her precious eggs. Though she and her mate circled and cried in protest, there was little she could do but return to what was left to continue her sitting.

Through wind, storm, rain, and gentle sunshine, the waiting continues until at last some new goslings peck through their tough shells. Mama Goose and her mate will not waste time doing what is best for their babies. One by one, they will tumble them down the hill to the safety of the water below.

She sits on her high perch day by day, a quiet lesson to all the human mamas. Though cold winds of adversity blow, we must stay home and guard our own. Though small interruptions ruffle our feathers, we need to calmly wipe noses, blow the ouchies, and cuddle the tired babies. When the gentle sun coaxes us to abandon all, to walk the forest paths, or to read page after page of our new book, we will quietly turn to those that depend on us to wash the dishes and laundry, stir the soup, and keep the floor swept. Always being there to seek what is best with a quiet song in our hearts, knowing that this is where we belong. Then, as the sun sets and the day cools, to gaze up and sing praises to the Giver for this ordinary, beautiful day.

For my thirtieth birthday, my sisters put a quilt in a frame and invited the Kuepfer cousins in to quilt, visit, and eat. Since then, each glimpse of my lovely quilt reminds me of that wonderful day and the message it speaks to me. The quilt is filled with lovely blue flowered circles linking over a white background. Just like those flowery links, my friends joined around the quilt, blossoming from each other's friendship and helping hands.

Let's keep our circles strong and our flames bright. The lovely quilt with its silent message still speaks to me.

• • •

"God answers prayer in a thousand different ways . . ."

I cling to this new thought. It is great comfort for the times we are sure our prayers went unheeded. With so many ways for prayers to be answered, it is no wonder we often do not, or cannot, see the answer. It might be kept hidden, sometimes until the future, sometimes forever. Or maybe we ignore the answer because it doesn't suit us. Perhaps it is simply "no" or "wait." Occasionally we might even be camouflaging our answer with the word *coincidence*.

One summer, a prize was being offered by a favorite magazine of mine. Not just any ordinary prize, but a rare find. *One Thousand Beautiful Things*, the volume was titled. "An old book, in great condition," the editor described it, filled with one thousand beautiful poems, stories, and quotes.

I knew a book like that would be gold on my shelf. I also knew my weak ink could not compete with the great pens of today. Yet I decided I could use the subject for my next essay to my writing teacher. She replied immediately with these orders: Revise and rewrite. Get a friend's input. Submit promptly to the aforementioned contest.

There wasn't much to lose, I decided. The article was already written, and revising was fun. I wouldn't be there to see the editor toss it aside and reach for her stack of more fluently written essays. At least I'd have the satisfaction of reporting to my mentor that I'd followed her instructions.

Besides, there on the couch sat Janelle, my niece. She'd work for the contest's requirement of a friend's input. She merely raised her eyebrows after the reading. With a smile, she commented, "I didn't know you were that interested in writing." That was all the input I needed. I stuffed the papers into an envelope and raced to beat the mail lady.

There was hardly time to blink in the weeks ahead, and certainly none for pondering the results of the contest. There were church services to host, the garden to clear, and the last of the veggies to cook, puree, and can. Meanwhile, deliverymen were piling winter wear inside the shoe store entryway and folks were eager to buy it. Somewhere, I lost myself to the petty things in life, and allowed challenging life events to color my world gray.

It was nearing lunchtime that memorable day as Eric and I rushed from the store to the mailbox. Slowly he reached in, pulling each envelope out one by one.

"Mom, there's a heavy package here," he announced.

Puzzled, I helped him tug it from the box. It bore the return address of a familiar magazine. The great pens had not bothered to enter the contest after all, I suddenly realized.

"It's my prize!" I screeched. Eric's small legs churned as I pulled him to the house.

There on the couch sat Janelle, unexpectedly there to share in the joy of the thick book's musty smell and beautiful readings. Readings that reconnect you with reality and the important things of life. Truly, *One Thousand Beautiful Things*.

• • •

I enjoyed her weekly columns. She touched on numerous subjects but always returned to her favorite one: hope. She was an encourager, forcing the reader to see the silver lining. It wasn't until after her death that her son shared the inside story with her readers. Not only did she point out the silver lining of the clouds to others, but she also had found that compensation on her own.

Already plagued with many health issues, she broke her ankle shortly after the death of her husband. It left her immobile and in a nursing home. During this dark time, she didn't let go of hope. It inspired her to get up and walk again. Best of all, she shared this hope with the nurses and patients. Soon the nurses would fetch her to share her hope with other depressed patients. When she returned home, she left a card with her number, just in case someone needed a listening ear.

How noble! As Proverbs 25:11 says, "A word fitly spoken is like apples of gold in pictures of silver."

If we all spoke hope, kindness, and cheer, how much better our world would be. I would start in my home, I resolved. Surely my children, husband, and even I would benefit from more hope and kindness.

I soon found that to speak hope, cheer, and kindness, one must first think hope, cheer, and kindness. That requires practice. Especially by one with deeply ingrained thought patterns of hurry, hurry, hurry and "What must be done next?" With four young children, these thought patterns make ideal breeding grounds for impatient words and quick, rash actions.

One day I needed some routine blood work. I discovered how much practice I still needed at spreading hope and cheer. The clinic I chose is notoriously busy, but prompt. The nurses in charge run a tight ship in a small space. The "hurry, hurry, get this done" environment frequently causes taut nerves and sharp words.

The morning started well enough. But as I whiled away the hour between my two blood draws, things began to fall apart.

It started with a tiny granny who had to watch the floor while she walked. She soon learned that the desk was not the spot she needed to hobble to.

"If you come to the window, I'll help you," the nurse at the desk said sharply. "See, there's a sign here that tells you that."

"Oh," murmured the granny, bravely lifting her head from her stooped shoulders to peer at the sign above. She nervously poked around her purse for the papers the nurse demanded from her.

The hour was up. My name was called and I was led to the last available cubicle. I soon found out the little old lady wasn't the only one who raised the nurses' ire. Routine questioning began.

"Did you eat or drink anything besides water today?" At the shake of my head, the nurse paused long enough to protest, "You don't need to fast for this test."

I tried to keep my voice light as I asked, "Did they change things recently?"

"No," she insisted. "You never had to fast for this test."

Remembering that I always had to fast for this test, I tried again. "Maybe the fasting was for the blood work they took earlier this morning?"

Very loudly and slowly, and in a tone used for small children, hard-of-hearing grannies, or uncooperative patients, I was asked, "Did you eat or drink anything today?"

"No," I replied, biting my tongue and desperately wishing I were a woman who could speak hope and cheer.

Just as the needle slid under my skin, there was an eruption in the hall. As quickly as possible, I was hustled from the room and directed to a row of chairs. There I sat with the other bewildered patients while the nurses held an angry, whispered conference. Apparently, one of the nurses had disrupted the steady flow of clients. I stared helplessly at the exasperated faces and waving hands as each tried to reclaim her schedule. By that time I had completely forgotten about hope and cheer. I wanted to jump up and shout, "Stop it, ladies. Grow up. Act professional."

At this part of the story, Allan teased, "So you were just like the rest of them? It must have been time for the group of you to go for lunch."

• • •

Our little household runs at its usual interesting pace. It seems Kyle has developed his mother's habit of telling long stories. At a pause during one of them, his sister, plainly bored, asked, "Is that the end of the story?"

"Oh no," he reassured her. "There's still more stuff in it."

Alyssa is trying to earn a ten-colors-of-ink-all-in-one pen, just like the one I loved when I was a child, by memorizing her addition and subtraction facts to 10. The pen is here in the house already, and has even been used occasionally. She is getting close to adding it to her stack of treasures.

The week of Easter holidays always bring a wonderful change in school routine for everyone before they finish the term. The last day is usually in mid-June. We keep our parochial schedule fairly consistent with the public schools, filling the quota of 186 school days.

Eric finally learned to color. We laughed when we reviewed his hurried scribbles, of any color, all over the page from the previous winter. Now he colors slowly and stays within the lines. The pictures are all colored the right colors. Sometimes Mom just needs to step back and let things correct themselves.

Bad dreams were on the rise when Mom and Dad graduated to a queen-size mattress. The little dreamers took full advantage of our extra space. Funny how they are never quite sure what their bad dreams were about. Snuggling with Mom and Dad soon soothes them back to sleep.

PART IV

Of Blankies
and Band-Aids

20

Sights, Smells, and Stories of Fall

ONE WEEK MY CURIOSITY got me a waffle iron and garden huckleberries.

"I'm going to get me a waffle iron with some Christmas gift money," my cousin informed me.

Forgetting to hide my ignorance, I asked, "Don't you need electricity to run one of those?"

But no, apparently not—they make stove-top ones.

That had my curiosity aroused. Would they really work properly on our wood-burning cookstoves? "What do you think?" I asked Delilah.

"Sure they do. I have one. Here, take it home and try it for a while," she generously offered.

The waffles were delicious with Ontario maple syrup. On Sunday we had waffles with strawberries and ice cream. But it was time to give the iron back.

Now about the huckleberries: they were just all right, and a learning experience for all of us.

Those came because of a usual autumn question I ask the lady customers at the shoe store. Is your garden plowed? One woman's reply was not so usual: normally it would be, she said, but we still didn't have any hard frosts to ripen the garden huckleberries. Garden huckleberries? Now what's that? She spent a few minutes sharing some information. They are annuals that grow on bushes. You need a hard frost to ripen the purple berries, which have a unique flavor. She left with the promise to bring me some.

The berries arrived, and they *were* purple! When you eat them you are guaranteed purple lips, purple teeth, and a purple tongue. If there are little ones around, there will be purple clothes, tablecloth, chairs, and floors as well. I'm thinking they must use them to color those juices and candies that declare boldly NO ARTIFICIAL FLAVORS AND COLORS and yet look and taste completely artificial.

She said she thickens them, adds blue Jell-O, and they eat the berries like that. I was sure they'd be good in pie. No one took a second piece, but we ate it.

• • •

It was that type of evening. The kind that relaxes you after a long, busy week. Kyle was still just a baby. The sunset brilliantly promised a few more hours of daylight while a full moon prepared to climb in the east. The distant honka-honka-honk of the Canada geese stirred the hunter's blood, and Allan casually remarked, "I think I'll go huntin' till dark."

"Me too! Me too!" the chorus sounded. "Please, Dad, please, me too!"

Doubtfully Dad eyed his little girl and boy and shook his head at the baby. "Well, if you can be quiet enough. Dress warmly, as it's going to be a chilly one."

Loud cheers answered him and no time was wasted grabbing coats and boots.

"We'll walk a far ways and it'll be the last time they'll want to go goose hunting," he grinned impishly at me as they left.

The poor baby did not easily forget his disappointment at being left behind. He took care of my idea of a relaxing evening. Darkness fell as I bathed him, dressed him in snuggly pajamas, and read aloud his favorite books. Still the goose hunters had not returned.

That far walk must not be going so well on the way home, I surmised as I settled into the rocker.

Suddenly the quiet was shattered. "Look! Look! We got one! We got one! Here's the bullet that got it. Feel its soft feathers. Look, Kyle, look!"

While we properly admired their fine goose, Dad told the story. They had walked for a long time along the old railway track. He was suspicious of geese landing in a field over yonder, so everyone started to crawl. Presently they came to a huge rock that the children quickly claimed as a rest area while Dad continued his stalking.

When the flock rose from the field, Dad squeezed off a shot. With satisfaction he watched a bird drop back to earth. Quickly sneaking a peek at the children to check their reaction, he lost his vantage point. By the time he refocused, the goose had landed. He walked back to the children to tell them he was going over to the cornfield to search for his goose.

"It's right there, Dad," they said, pointing several yards in front of them.

That night before Alyssa went to bed she sighed and said, "Every time Dad goes goose hunting, I'm going too."

"Me too," Eric agreed.

• • •

When Alyssa first started going to school, she had lunch pail dilemmas. Nothing worked well for her, so finally she just packed her lunch into a small backpack. That was, until she found the perfect solution. "Mom," she announced one day after school, "there are girls at school with a little cooler for a lunch pail. They told me you buy them at the Home Hardware store in Milverton."

She planned everything, even mentally picking the blue one instead of red. There was no passing the hardware store the next time we clopped to town with Mabel. There we found an array of lunch pails on the shelf, but no little square coolers. "Oh, look here, Alyssa," I said. "There's an empty spot here and the tag reads 'Coleman coolers.'"

I noted that the price tag explained the reason for the many little coolers at school. It was easily the most economical purchase at the store.

"We'll ask the clerk," I consoled my disappointed daughter. "Maybe she'll have more somewhere."

She did not, but she knew the product well and offered to order us one.

When the long-awaited day came to pick up our purchase, the clerk reached behind the counter. "Here you go," she announced cheerfully. The little blue cooler was just what we wanted, except the name on the tag was that of a parent of one of Alyssa's schoolmates! The friendly clerk soon found the box with our name on it, and we were on our way, little blue lunch pail in hand.

The first morning of the little blue lunch box, she packed her own lunch. When she finished, she giggled, "My mom slept in while I made lunch"—a line from a poem we both enjoy.

"But it was a healthy one!" she quickly added, in a nod to the poet's unhealthy lunch description.

When Alyssa was a preschooler, she cut, colored, pasted, wrote, painted, and taped her days away. Eric would have none of it. His tractors roared while his sheep bleated for hay. When Alyssa went off to school, Eric took up her role. His scissors snipped endlessly and his glue sticks were always empty. Little brother Kyle, on the other hand, was too busy baling big round bales to pay much attention to his brother. So it goes.

21

Turkey in a Hole

ALLAN WAS RELIEVED. I finally had a *good* story to write about.

Opening morning of the turkey hunt he got up extra early. To his chagrin, it wasn't to go hunting but to get an early start at work. Unexpectedly, his crew finished their job by midafternoon. There was no doubt about how he would spend his free hours! There were a lot of fine details to the next part of the story, which involved calling, strutting, gobbling, and a BANG! You'll have to ask Allan if you want to know more about that part of it. In less than an hour, he was a happy hunter with a nineteen-pound turkey with a nine-inch beard.

I told Allan and the children to invite some company and I'd try the wild turkey recipe my mother found for me. First of all, the hunter always prepares the meat at this house. I'll repeat, *always*! Then Mom does the cooking. Maybe I'm too strict about that part, for when we were checking the roasting bird, three-year-old Eric said, "Dad shoot a turkey!" and then quickly added, "But Mom cook it!"

I started by placing the bird on the rack of my largest roasting pan and quartered two large apples into the cavity. Next

I sliced two onions around it and added two cups of water. I rubbed the turkey with one and a half teaspoons seasoned salt, one teaspoon pepper, and one teaspoon salt. For the basting sauce, I mixed a half cup maple syrup, a quarter cup French salad dressing, a quarter cup barbecue sauce, two tablespoons ketchup, two tablespoons steak sauce, and one tablespoon lemon juice. I brushed that combination over the turkey, and covered it. I had to use large sheets of tinfoil, as the long legs pushed my roaster lid off. It takes at least three and a half hours at 325 degrees Fahrenheit before the meat is tender. I accidentally had my chimney draft open while I was baking mine, so my heat was rising up the chimney instead of heating my oven. By suppertime, only the breasts were tender, but that was plenty of meat. The dog ended up eating the long, tough legs.

We had enough meat left over to feed a long tableful of company the next day. Then I made hot turkey-and-cheese sandwiches, and the meal after that was turkey soup. Finally Allan asked if he was going to eat turkey forever!

The turkey hunt is fairly new to this area, but there is a good supply of turkeys. I enjoy this hunt too, as it fits well with our lifestyle. The hunts are early morning or late afternoon.

• • •

The next time Allan shot a turkey we decided to cook it outside. We dug a hole three feet deep and three feet wide. Next, we built a fire in it with good, solid hardwood. After six man-sized armloads of wood and three hours, the hole was three-quarters full of glowing coals. I rubbed the wild turkey with salt, pepper, and butter, and stuffed the innards with ice. Then we wrapped it in seven layers of heavy-duty, twenty-four-inch tin-foil. We secured it with wire, leaving one end dangling. Some of the coals were raked aside, and we set the tinfoil-encrusted bird in the pit of glowing coals. More coals were raked on top, and then we finished by covering everything with soil. We kept the dangling wire poking out for an easier way to pull up the finished turkey. There! We'd done everything the instructions told us to do. Now all I needed was seven hours of faith. Would I have fowl to grace our company table, or would we be eating canned sausage?

When the allotted cooking time was up, everyone (company included) trooped back to fetch the main dish. I held my breath as they started digging. Soon a few tugs on the wire freed the bird. I gasped to see the juices running out of one corner. Were they red? A quick peek under the tinfoil revealed a well-done bird. Whew! Breathe out!

The meat was too well done, we learned at supper. Sister Kathryn, the cook, says it was because we skinned it. Skinned fowl cooks faster. We'll file that tip for next time. Will there be a next time? Time will tell, but I think so.

• • •

At our house turkey means rising before daylight and sitting for hours in cold, heat, or mosquitoes. Patience, Allan, and his gun have rewarded us with many fine meals.

Allan decided it was time Mom—*me*—got in on the fun. He borrowed his boss's two-person pop-up tent, so there were no mosquitoes to worry about. Mommy Over There was coaxed into babysitting, so no worries there either. I agreed to go, so the alarm was set.

That was before the baby woke up numerous times that night with teething problems. By the time the alarm sounded, I was ready to turn over and sleep. I wished I hadn't when I awoke at daybreak to a loud kaboom!

Mom wasn't a necessary ingredient for keeping the roast pan filled.

22

Way Back in the Day

I'VE ENJOYED HEARING and watching each of the children develop their vocabularies. Alyssa especially enjoys gathering new words and trying them out. One night her new word was *material*. She was scolding her little brother for touching the "material" she had just gotten. What he was really touching was her new book, so I don't think she had her definition quite right.

The squirrels were helping themselves to the walnuts and providing a lot of entertainment for us. After observing a squirrel sitting up and eating his breakfast nut, Alyssa asked, "Mom, is he praying?"

• • •

When Eric had his first haircut at fifteen months, it was a true family affair. Daddy held his hands. Mom had the scissors and Alyssa held the ziplock bag to catch the trimmings. When it was all over, she peered into the bag. "But I can't see anything!" she cried in dismay. We kept the whole cutting for his baby book.

We took the children to the small local stockyards where Uncle David works. Just some pigs and calves being sold to a handful of buyers, but it was as good as a zoo to them. "When you get to be a big farmer like Uncle David, you may work here too," Alyssa assured Eric. His eyes sparkled and danced. I think he liked that idea.

• • •

Alyssa was happy when I handed out butter rum Lifesavers—until she tasted them. "Today at church Dad gave me colorful ones," she announced. "I just can't eat this rotten one," she said, handing it back.

• • •

Alyssa, being a typical little girl, wants everything to be purple. Purple dress, purple cup, purple candies, and even purple vitamin pills. Eric, at age one and a half, already associated purple with the concept that purple is something nice, good, or the thing you want. "Purple, purple," he pleaded many times a day. Standing in front of the sink whining "Me, me, purple" meant he needed a drink.

Pointing to where he once saw Mom getting candy and coaxing "Purple, purple" was a hopeful wish for more.

A dazed, heavy-lidded boy sighing "Purple, Purple" meant he was most likely searching for his fuzzy, blue night-night blankie.

• • •

I think we should all have a friend like Purple. He's always there. When you're sad, when Mom's not around, or if you're tired, Purple always comforts. Just hold him, fuzzy and blue, against your face, and everything feels so much better. His only fault is that he's frequently dirty and it takes all day to wash and dry him. But when bedtime comes, there he is all fuzzy and sweet smelling. Ah, Purple.

Eric could often be found scratching his dry, scaly eczema patches. It would flare up when the woodstove dried the air too much. He would relax contentedly whenever I rubbed his itchy legs with moisturizer.

"Uh-huh, uh-huh," he murmured, nuzzling Purple.

Once after I finished, he poked his finger under his sock, "Right there," he requested. It would do no good to let Mom miss even one tiny itchy spot.

• • •

One year we had a green January. Perfect for pond and puddle skating—whenever the temperature dipped low enough. I had a welcome message one Friday afternoon that January. Leons' invited us for supper and to skate. I informed the children. In no time this information fired up Alyssa.

"Eric," she stated, "Dad and I will skate. Mom won't because then the ice would crack. You'd better not either, just in case."

"Me want to swim too," Eric pouted.

• • •

They say tomorrow never comes; well, it did at our house. One morning when I went to fetch Eric from his crib, he popped up and announced, "Now it's tomorrow."

Tomorrow was exciting because Mommy, Daddy, and Uncle David were going to Pennsylvania for three days. The day had barely begun before Eric started crying for Mommy. That was unusual. After prodding a bit he finally confessed. "Me want a piece of bubble gum," he pouted.

• • •

One day when Kyle was just four months old, I was just sitting on the couch. Just sitting. I wasn't holding anyone, reading, writing, or hand sewing. I was just sitting. Alyssa glanced over and remarked, "Mom, you look so content."

"Thou wilt keep him in perfect peace, whose mind is stayed on thee," goes the verse in Isaiah 26. Perhaps Alyssa caught that vision of happy peace.

• • •

Cousin Jarred announced, "Daddy is Paul." Mommy Far Away decided to test Eric's knowledge with, "What is *your* daddy's name?"

He hesitated a minute before replying, "Daddy dear."

• • •

Uncle Dougs' are sheep farmers. That means we've had opportunities to taste all things sheep: sheep milk, sheep cheese, and once, sheep ice cream. I guess this is what Alyssa had in mind when she tasted the pear sauce they sent over. "Hmm," she said, "Mom, is this apple or sheep?"

• • •

Our children still delight in new words and expressions. Eric's latest is "way back in the day."

He saw an old baby carriage in Doddy's shop. "Dad," he said, waving his hand toward it, "I bet that way back in the day that was yours."

Another time, while in the same shop, a wise thought struck him and he immediately passed his wisdom on. "Way back in the day all this stuff was new and there were no old-fashioned things."

And once I left him patiently waiting in the kitchen while I had a shower. Unfortunately, the battery died, and the light with it. When I returned he was quietly waiting in the dark.

"Were you scared?" I questioned.

"Yes," he whispered.

"But nothing got you," I pointed out.

"Oh no," he replied, "they're all in the wild."

• • •

I finally got to work on some projects that had been waiting.

First of all was Doddy (Joseph K.) Albrecht's book. The book was actually given to Mommy Albrecht, my grandmother, to write in. It is in the form of a daily journal with a question to answer each day. After Mommy passed away without writing one word in it, Doddy spent hours filling it out in his faltering, Parkinson's hand. It is a keeper. I sorted notes and started to recopy. Eventually I tired of working on it so I packed it up and sent it to Mom and my sisters. I'll see what's left to do when I get it back.

It almost frightens me to learn how much times have changed since Doddy's day, and he is not even seventy-five years older than I am! He told of a local farmer who went to the Massey-Harris tractor dealer and said he was going to get rid of his team of horses. Well, the dealer thought he'd better not do that. How would he cultivate his corn, travel to the bush, thresh his grain, and do the numerous other jobs that tractors are no good for? He wrote that each farmer had kept at least one good team.

Underneath "Learning to Drive," Doddy Albrecht wrote:

We had a big, four-year-old colt that was never led or driven, and a mare who tried to run away every chance she got. One morning Dad said that we were going to Wellesley to pick up some livestock and we'll take the mare and the colt. Sides were put on the wagon and the back was left open. The team was hitched up in an open field and Dad held them by their heads. He told me to take the lines, and when all is ready he'll jump on the back. After he jumped on I said, "You better take the reins."

He said, "You have them, drive." I didn't have much choice as we were already galloping around the field. We raced around the field a few times, and then headed to Wellesley. We got there and back without any trouble.

Doddy went on to note: "Never before, or since, have I driven with so little control. After that ride I was never afraid to drive anything else."

23

Purple Hands and New Teeth

ERIC WAS READY for a high chair but Alyssa still hadn't moved out, so I took some gift money and went shopping at a local furniture shop. I soon spied it. A high stool with a neat, rounded back. The perfect chair to which Alyssa could graduate.

One day we were having lunch in the usual way. Alyssa on her stool, Eric in the high chair, and me in between the two on Alan's usual chair. Suddenly Alyssa gave a quick shove backward and wham! Over she flew with the stool. The shriek she gave had me quickly inspecting each limb, but everything was fine. In the end I concluded that she had bit her tongue.

After they were tucked in for their naps, I heard her worried little voice. "Mom," she quivered, "I broke my tooth." And sure enough, her eyetooth was split up the middle.

The dentist said it had to come out. She was as brave as a two-year-old can be, and I was brave too! In no time at all there were two small pieces on the dentist's tray.

She jumped from her chair and cried, "Mom, is he going to give me another tooth?"

After we were at home she told me, "I'm going back to the dentist again."

"Oh," I said, very surprised.

"Yes, for my new tooth. But I won't sit on the long chair," she was quick to add.

. . .

That new high stool of Alyssa's caused other problems. I wasn't really listening the day Alyssa thoroughly explained how she got a little owie on her hand. I didn't look closely, either, when she showed the prized spot. All I said was "Uh-huh" when she asked if she might get a Band-Aid for it. One moment later I was back to reality. In that moment I knew just how the grandpa felt in the poem: "Grandpa dropped his glasses once in a pot of dye, and when he put them on again he saw a purple sky." But my glasses weren't at fault and there my daughter stood, dejectedly wringing hands dripping with purple dye.

The bathroom looked just as I had feared. There was purple antiseptic dripping from the new stool to the floor, and a big splat had hit the white wall, the sink, and just about everything else in the tiny room. After that first moment of being frozen in horror, I sprang into action. I seized what was left of the bottle of gentian violet and threw it in the stove. Then I wiped. I scrubbed. I rubbed. I repeated those actions. Finally, after naptha fluid, Comet, and all-purpose cleaner, there still were dull, purple stains. Alyssa gazed sadly at her hands. "Dad will know from my hands," she mourned. It must have healed the owie, as we never did get that Band-Aid put on.

24

Somebody Follows You

SOMEBODY FOLLOWS YOU. We're reminded of this over and over. Yet during the daily grind we tend to ignore the fact. After all, there's nothing about me that anyone would want to copy. Beware! You might have more followers than you will ever realize! Let me explain.

Just recently Alyssa was carefully examining every inch of her smooth, dark-skinned leg. Her search ended when she found a tiny blemish. "Mom, look," she happily sighed. "Just like Aunt Laura's legs."

I knew her legs were a far cry from Aunt Laura's eczema-riddled, itchy legs, but Alyssa was happy. At least one of her legs was well on the way to looking like Aunt Laura's. Once she colored her fingernails bright red because the ladies at the bank do. I believe she missed the fact that they don't use their mother's fabric markers to do the job.

• • •

Itchy skin problems seem to run in my family. One day I was washing the buggy in our warm shop. Allan moved a pile of dusty planks and swept up the dust. That was enough to provoke the skin on my face, neck, hands, and arms. By next morning I had an angry, red rash. Soon it began to swell. "An allergic reaction," the doctor said. "Just be glad you weren't wearing a bikini!"

So I itched and scratched and scratched and itched. My skin peeled and people scratched just from looking at me. Three weeks later I was okay except for my hands. They had no chance to heal because they were always in water: dishwater, laundry water, or scrub water. When they were out of water, they were holding wet face cloths.

They peeled, itched, and cracked, so I rubbed them with Glaxal Base, and Vaseline, and B&W salve. I scratched and scratched until I was glad to swallow an allergy pill, even if it made me feel like half a person. I resolved to start wearing rubber gloves and never, ever a bikini.

• • •

Naomi over at the bulk food store knows how to give good deals. One day she treated four-year-old Alyssa to one. When the door flew open and Alyssa bounced in, proudly showing her pocketful of nickels and dimes that were going to pay the bill, Naomi tactfully stated, "I'll have to give you a deal."

All Alyssa heard was that Naomi was giving her something. That something was going to be a deal. She was sure Naomi went to get it when she ran to the house. No, it was just seasoning salt she was fetching. When it was time for us to leave, Alyssa dutifully reminded Naomi that she still hadn't given her a deal. Because she wasn't successful at explaining the meaning of deal, Naomi reached for a horse notepad and, pulling off one page, wrote on it: "a deal."

Alyssa happily put her deal in her pocket, and that night at supper she announced, "Dad, today Naomi gave me a deal. A deal is a piece of paper with a horse picture and some writing on it," she explained.

At least no one lost money with that deal.

• • •

Alyssa always liked to talk. At two days old, her new dad had laid her on the table in front of him and softly cooed to her. She watched intently with her small, dark eyes. Finally, he was rewarded with a soft, delightful gurgle.

It didn't stop. By the time she was one and a half years old, she had mastered sentences and could clearly pronounce all words except *squirrel*. We distinctly remember this, as it was one of the first words that caused her difficulty!

Eric wasn't quite as quick with words, or so we thought. By his second birthday he was chattering as well as his big sister. My book *What to Expect in the Toddler Years* informed us that some children are genetically programmed to speak as clearly as adults long before they are three years old.

Those genetics didn't touch our baby Kyle. He was one quiet spot in our noisy household. Vigorously his head would shake no if we'd suggest he repeat a word.

After our oldest, I often wondered how parents felt if their toddlers didn't talk. I figured they'd probably worry. How would you know if your baby was developing properly? Would you know what they wanted or how much they really understood?

No worries. The nontalkers take things into their own hands. What they lack in words they fill with facial expressions and sign language. A pat on the cheek and a loving smile say as much as any "I love you." Same for the "Mama-Daddy, Mama-Daddy" chant Kyle was fond of. As for how much he understood, there are ways of getting that across too.

One morning he stood on Dad's glider to watch "Joe" the squirrel enjoy his breakfast at the bird feeder. Suddenly, Kyle clasped his hands, squinted his eyes and prayed his version of the children's table prayer "*Helf, helf, helf.*"—"Help, help, help."

"Are you praying, Kyle?" I asked.

He nodded yes, smiling mischievously.

"Why?" I questioned further.

"That," he replied, pointing at the busy squirrel.

Then I saw what he saw: a squirrel with paws clasped, praying over a tray of seeds. The sunflower seed was too tiny to see and the jaws might be just as busy praying as eating.

Around his second birthday he decided to develop his own vocabulary. It was a strange one, making sense only to him and his little family.

"Golli-gitti" he'd cry when a tractor passed on the road.

"Gum-de-gums" gave him all the food and drink he needed.

Finally, at age two and a half, his vocabulary began growing by leaps and bounds. Thankfully, it was the same one we used! He often found at least one word to repeat from our sentences. Soon he started to string those words together.

"Dad, home; Rich, work?" he asked one day. I knew what he really meant was "Is Dad at home with Rich from work?"

We'd soon have to remind him, "Shh, let's eat instead of talking."

• • •

Young boys and girls can be a big help to their moms. Sweeping floors, washing or drying dishes, cleaning sinks and windows, filling the woodbox, and watering flowers are all favorite jobs at our house. The same old over and over can get tiring, though. That's when the children's cookbook comes out.

We were delighted when Alyssa chose to make "Simple Muffins" one Saturday. (The recipe can be found in the recipe section at end of this book.) We broke them in half and spread butter and jam on them. Alyssa knew they were delicious, as there were only two left.

• • •

Our children use arguing for a pastime, I think. They even argue about imaginary things. Ever the peacemaker, I would offer suggestions like "Let's have two mothers and no daddy" or "Isn't it okay for Alyssa to have a Standardbred and Eric can drive a Haflinger?" Contentment generally reigns only for a few minutes before there are more details to iron out.

One morning, Eric announced that he would be the daddy and Kyle would be the boy. Kyle protested bitterly to this familiar role. "No, no, me daddy. You boy," he demanded, pointing to Eric.

"We could have more than one daddy the way we have many at church," I suggested.

"But, Mom," rose Eric's protest, "Kyle doesn't even know how to read a newspaper right. He just scatters it all over instead of reading it. You can't be a daddy if you can't read the paper."

• • •

In Kyle's journey to independence, I remember these steps.

"I will self," he would say, and pulled the wagonload of fishing poles and older siblings.

"Own," he'd announce, and served himself dinner.

"Me too," he proclaimed, and pushed the lawn mower over the grass with no gears running.

He put on his own coat and boots. He could find his own blanket, crawl up the stairs, and onto Mom's lap on the rocking chair, *all by himself.*

I'm certain he won't leave home to live on his own anytime soon, though. He still hasn't managed to change his own diaper, nor to rock and sing himself to sleep.

• • •

Shortly after my wedding, my sister and I were discussing cleaning days when our siblings were young and we were all at home. It was the knife that held our attention. Definitely not your usual cleaning tool. We always made use of it, though, to clean the high chair and floor around it. Thinking of it, my sister and I just shook our heads and grinned. I even secretly wondered what kind of housekeeper our mother really was.

Not anymore. The other day I got a sharp paring knife and carefully scraped dried food from baby's high chair and the floor around it. I sighed as I looked at the state of my house and thought of the little verse: "Cleaning house when the children are young is like shoveling the walk before the snowing is done."

I don't sigh quite so hopelessly anymore. I learned there are two kinds of dirt—old dirt and new dirt. There's a difference, stated an article I read. That's why my house isn't so hopeless. I don't have to make sure there's *no* dirt. Just that the dirt doesn't get too old. And when it does I can always use a knife.

PART V

It's a Small World

25

Kittens and Good Mothers

"THEY'RE IN HERE," Alyssa said, leading the very clean, sophisticated-looking woman to my washhouse.

"They're so cute!" the lady exclaimed.

"Mom, these kittens are so cute!"

My humiliation made me blurt out, "But I don't even like kittens."

"Well, you're a good mom then," the woman announced.

A good mom? How could she say that? She was standing there in my washhouse littered with kittens, wood shavings, dirty clothes, and grubby children.

But she wasn't interested in her surroundings. All her attention was directed on Alyssa and her kittens. She was telling me mothering is not just about keeping your children and washhouse clean. Some of it is about allowing kittens in your washhouse when you simply can't stand kittens.

• • •

I hated shivering in bed, under a pile of covers, in the middle of the day. I hated it more that Allan and the children went to church without me. I thought it terrible that Eric went to church with a cap that was missing its strings. I couldn't find his other one. Allan thought it fit well with the picture of going to church without a mama. I was sorry to miss out on Eileen's good supper and company. Alyssa was too. Later while eating supper she announced, "Here it's suppertime and it's Sunday and we didn't go to Keith and Eileen's."

But I coped. After all, it was just the flu. You do get better if it's just the flu. Besides that, it was wonderful that Allan was brave enough to take the older children to church by himself. The baby and I were delighted to sleep the morning away. And I was at home. Where is a better spot to be if you don't feel well? I thought there was a strong chance of getting another invitation from Eileen. And someone had dropped Eric's missing cap in the mailbox. No, it wasn't as bad as I thought.

• • •

Uncle Jody was always the envy of my little boys and girl. He had cages filled with pigeons, quails, and ducks. A flock of banties and chickens with beautiful stripes and speckles that pecked and scratched where they pleased. Trips to Doddys', where Uncle Jody also lived, always contained the pleasure of checking the frequently changing contents of the cages. Doddy had one pet, a stray housecat, that the grandchildren named Stripes. She lived contentedly in a box in Doddy's metal shop. One evening when we stopped in at Doddys' there were four tiny, mewing kittens in the box with Stripes! Then Doddy's shop got a visit before Jody's pet cages!

During one visit to Doddys', Eric and Alyssa plotted to ask Dad and Mom if they could buy some of Jody's pigeons.

"Please, please," Alyssa begged. "They won't take much room and we'll feed them every day."

"Yes, *please*," Eric chorused.

There was then-two-year-old Kyle standing beside them, nose wrinkled, and eyes silently pleading.

"Did you want a pigeon too, Kyle?" I asked.

He quickly shook his head. "Kitty," he begged.

26

No Empty Cages

CAGES SHOULDN'T BE EMPTY. Dad and Mom said, "No pets" so the boys found their own way to fill the cage. Catch a squirrel.

Eric begged Doddy and Uncle David's help to set two live traps. The blue jays' peanuts were the bait. For four days the squirrels kept their distance. Each night Eric closed his window tight. He didn't want to hear the snap of the trap's lid.

But the lid never snapped.

Then, Saturday afternoon on the way to the blacksmith, Eric cried, "Turn back, turn back! There's something in the trap!"

His dad noticed that the squirrel was very still, but the excited Eric paid no attention. Carefully, he reached in for the prize. He held it high in disgust. "Those Dannys' boys," he laughed as he tossed a stuffed puppy on the lawn.

That's when his dad suggested he let the squirrels be. "They are just too smart," he told him. "They won't let you catch them anyway."

His dad's lack of faith and the stuffed puppy fueled his determination. Monday morning he set the bait higher. "I'll catch one today. I will! I will!" he said as we left for town.

Traps and squirrels had fled my mind as I put Mabel in her stall and unloaded the groceries. But not for long. Shouts of "We caught a squirrel! We caught a squirrel!" rang over the neighborhood.

This squirrel was not quiet. It gave angry shrieks as it whirled around the trap. A black streak was all we saw when the trap's door was lifted. At lunchtime Eric ended the exciting tale with a happy sigh. "Dad said we'd never catch one but we did. Let's go after a tomcat next."

27

The Puppy Mom Never Wanted

WE FINALLY GOT A PUPPY in 2011! It was major news, right up there with the 2011 Canadian elections and William and Kate's royal wedding, I think.

He was black and white with a smudge of brown, and wiggly and cute like all puppies are. His name was Georgie and he hogged all the attention from Mom those days.

I was definitely not sure about it all, and here's why: I don't really care for dogs. But there was a spot in my mother heart that just melted and gave in to the puppy idea.

One evening, a glance out of the window revealed a dog and a girl seated side by side, silhouetted against the evening sky. As I watched, the girl suddenly leaned over and kissed the dog. That must have pleased the dog, as it didn't move a muscle. There was time for one more kiss and a hug before the dog's master came galloping along on his pony. The girl gazed longingly after the pony, the boy, and his dog as they disappeared around the bend before she raced to the kitchen.

"Mom, Mom, smell this cheek," she instructed. "Not this one, just this one."

And I knew what I should say: "Ah, it smells like a puppy."

So we looked forward to a summer of a puppy and a boy: to keep them off the road, out of the flower beds, and wherever else puppies and boys go that they shouldn't.

• • •

"The puppy, the puppy! Mom, the puppy!"

Georgie was acting just as puppies act. He chewed, nipped, jumped, and dug in flower beds. Neighbor Sarah Anne said cayenne pepper keeps puppies out of flower beds, but not boys.

Eric picked grass stems and fed them to Georgie. Georgie obediently grabbed and chewed them. They must be good if Georgie ate them. Soon they were pulled from Georgie's mouth and Eric took his turn at chewing them.

• • •

We also rescued kitties at times. Once there wasn't one but two kitties in need of rescuing. The first lucky feline was in desperate need of a bath, so the nearest water puddle did the trick. A sunny spot on the wagon made the perfect dryer. After Alyssa had her snack time, she checked on the kitty and found an empty wagon with Georgie beside it busily chewing a bone. Loud wails erupted, punctuated by "*Mom, Mom, Georgie ate my kitty!*"

Georgie, looking as guilty as condemned, started chewing faster and tried to quickly swallow the last of his bone.

That time it wasn't just the girlie who was washed with relief when Mom spied the kitty in the flower bed.

• • •

For a time, I said Eric didn't have a mind of his own at two. He just used his big sister's. He didn't want ketchup on his sausage because she didn't. He colored and "wrote" a lot because she did. He asked "Why? Why?" because that's what she asked. He even used her reasons. "Can I go over to Doddys' Over There and tell them something?"

When it came to Purple, though, he was his own man. "Is Purple in the bag?" he would ask before we went away. At only four months old, baby brother picked up the habit too. There's just nothing more comforting then a fuzzy blanket tucked under the nose.

We were on our way to the shop to wash the muddy carriage when Eric's tummy rumbled.

"I need a snack," he announced. "And I will not let Georgie eat it," he added determinedly.

I put his cookie in a container and added a sprinkle of Fruit Loops as an extra treat. His brown eyes sparkled and once more he declared, "Georgie may not eat them, Mom."

When we reached the shop he scolded Georgie before Georgie even had a chance at the snack. "This snack is not for you, Georgie," he proclaimed. Things went well until I had to tend the furnace. When I returned, the cookie was gone and Eric was in tears. Georgie was wagging his tail. The children's book says dogs wag their tails to say thank you. If that's the case, at least we had a polite dog.

The tears turned to a smile when I reminded Eric of all the Fruit Loops he had left to eat. Once again he told me that he wouldn't let Georgie have the rest of his snack. But all the while Georgie had his nose in the container, slowly wagging his tail and crunching happily. Mom came to the rescue, but

Georgie still won. Most of the Fruit Loops were sacrificed to convince Georgie to do his tricks, sit, and shake a paw.

Oh, my little son. You are too often just like your Mom. So often I'm determined I will not fall again into my bad habits. Then again I am reminded how the spirit is willing, but the flesh is weak. Alone we cannot . . .

• • •

But Georgie the dog was not meant to be. He did not grow old alongside our children, as we had hoped he would. Maybe someday, a long time from now, we will get another dog. Maybe we will do a better job of training next time. For now, we will stay busy with our children.

28

Our Little Dolly

Lo, children are an heritage of the LORD: and the fruit of the womb is his reward.

—Psalm 127:3

IN APRIL OF 2015, we added a new baby to our growing family. Our whole world revolved around the new addition once again. Who held her last? Did she smile at me? Which of our neighbors, friends, or family put that good food on the table? Who is sending their willing girls to do our work? Are her eyes really blue? What? Supper isn't on the table yet and it's six o'clock! Oh, Mom's with the baby.

We named her Chloe Anne, and call her our "dolly." She weighed exactly what she should: seven pounds. That is exactly four ounces more than Kyle weighed at birth, who weighed four ounces more than Eric, who weighed four ounces more than six-pound-four-ounce baby Alyssa!

Alyssa floats on a cloud of delight now that she finally has a sister. She's sure her sister should never wear anything that isn't pink or purple. This isn't too difficult despite our stash of blue clothes. My mom and sisters were quite generous with gifts of cuddly pink sleepers, blankets, and socks. Baby Chloe is the first pink bundle in my family after a seven-year streak of blue!

Her big brother Kyle, with all his three years of wisdom, says, "She's a boy now. Just for a bit, until she gets braids hanging down." By the looks of her hair crops, there will be braids at a younger age than we're used to. Maybe she won't be a "boy" for too long.

Just like our others, her hair is dark, but it is quickly turning a few shades lighter. Like our others, she's a short, round bundle with a fat, round face and skin a few shades darker than her pale mother. Like our others, she has complete strangers asking, "Does she look like her dad?"

She brought a new twist to familiar looks though. When her face is beet red from the effort of waking, it highlights her white-blond eyebrows and eyelashes. And maybe her eyes have a sheen of blue? Perhaps she inherited some of her mother's looks instead of just her nature, as our others did? We'll tell you in a few years.

I think she's like the baby in the book my grandmother Kuepfer liked to read aloud to my siblings and me. The baby in the book also had two older brothers and a big sister.

One evening the children in this picture book were left with a babysitter. The gray-haired sitter was sure that the baby couldn't sleep while one big brother hammered together a birdhouse, the other listened to his radio and munched a peanut butter sandwich, and sister built a tower of blocks while loudly singing "Old MacDonald Had a Farm."

Shortly after Mrs. Sitter had quieted the children, the baby started crying. The sitter tried everything to quiet her. A bottle, diaper change, and a cuddly blanket did not stop the crying.

Finally, big brother suggested that the baby liked it when he listened to his radio. The other said she liked when he built his birdhouse. And sister was sure she liked her tower, song, and even the crash when the tower fell. After everyone went back to their former activities, the baby calmed. On the last page she was soundly asleep in her crib, calmed by all the noise.

That's our baby's story. Though her big sister sings lustily while rocking her, she keeps on sleeping. While Eric cuddles beside her, sharing bits of five-year-old wisdom, she slumbers on. And when her youngest brother squeezes and kisses her, all the while offering loud words of endearment, she merrily wiggles and yawns before continuing her sleep.

But that blissful sleep always ends as soon as we all leave the house. Even if I'm back in just a few minutes, she'll be wiggling and stretching, trying to wake. If we're out for more than a few minutes, we return to loud, urgent cries. Something tells me she likes the noise, singing, and squeezing.

"Real tractors," Kyle mused. "That's my bestest thing in the whole, wide world."

"No, Kyle," Eric quickly corrected him. "Our baby sister is."

I like to think about that. It reminds me of the disciples, who knew Jesus had great and important work to do. So they chased the mothers with their children away. Jesus noticed:

"Suffer little children, and forbid them not, to come unto me: for of such is the kingdom of heaven" (Matthew 19:14).

"Verily I say unto you, Whosoever shall not receive the kingdom of God as a little child shall in no wise enter therein" (Luke 18:17).

• • •

On rainy days I live among my pots, pans, bowls, and spoons. The children cook and bake. Each pot gets stirred and stirred. I don't think they ever burn anything! Those days I'm not Mom anymore, but "Emmaline," Alyssa's new name for me.

"Emmaline" hears all about raising babies, shopping, and running stores. All "Emmaline" has to do is to smile and nod her head.

PART VI

Garden of Plenty

29

Five Rows of Peas

MAY IS THE MONTH of soaring hopes for planters and hunters. The planters hope for a bountiful harvest and the hunters for a plump tom turkey for the dinner table.

For those of you unfamiliar with wild turkey history, wild turkeys actually became extinct in Canada because of mass killings by the early settlers and the clearing of forests. Allan says we have Americans to thank for the return of our turkeys. Michigan gave us turkeys in exchange for moose. Now, I don't suppose this was a pound-for-pound deal! We also traded river otter for turkeys with another state.

Now there are an estimated eighty thousand to one hundred thousand birds here in Canada. They must populate rapidly, as even ten years ago a turkey sighting in this area was rare. Now we see them in large flocks, feeding in the back fields.

A controlled spring hunt has been established. If two hundred bearded birds are killed in your area for three years in succession, you're given a fall hunt. In autumn you may hunt the hens as well. Before you head for the bush, you need a turkey hunting permit, which requires attending a Saturday seminar.

Pay the fee and answer a forty-question exam with less than five wrong, and you're good to go! Happy hunting!

I'll leave the hunting to the hunters and concentrate on the planting. Maybe I can coax my hunter for a hand now and again! Mommy Next Door and I traded our plots. I needed more and she needed less, so it was a good switch. I ordered a big box of seeds during the January blahs. Here was my list: carrots, beets, radishes, romaine and iceberg lettuce, rutabagas and turnips, yellow and green beans, corn, peas, dill, parsley, and "pie pumpkins" for the back corner.

I ordered enough cucumber seeds for a long row. I like to can at least twelve half-gallon jars of tiny, sweet dill pickles to use when church services are at our house. Of course we like some for ourselves, plus garlic dills, sour dills for Allan, and chunk pickles. We've had cucumber blight in this area for a number of years. Everyone is coming up with solutions. Mine is simply to plant lots of cucumbers so that I've picked our share before the blight hits. Once it hits, the game is usually over in a few days.

Of course, a garden for most Amish women isn't complete without flowers. I use the seeds I saved from last year's lovely blooms. Mini sunflowers, marigolds, zinnias, cosmos, and sweet peas should add color and bees.

Each year I enjoy trying something new. One year it was the summer squash that another *Connection* writer, Lena, often wrote of. I wasn't sure how my family would like it. I also tried spinach and cress. After testing, we decide whether they will join my garden goodies the next year.

Late in May I set out the pepper and tomato plants that I started in the house. I always protect the tender seedlings with plastic jugs with the bottoms cut off.

I usually plant potatoes. We had too many to use up one winter. I'll need to plant fewer and then keep a good eye out for the potato beetles.

I carry my big box of dead-looking geranium plants up from the cellar and happily plant scraggly plants with no leaves. In about a week the stalks start to show new leaf growth. Those that don't sprout end up on the manure heap.

About mid-June, we expect the first ripe strawberries. My bed has seventy-five plants, so I anticipate enough for our family, plus some to share.

Our nieces sent instructions for planting a garden with their secret valentine package. Perhaps you've read similar. First plant five rows of peas: preparedness, perseverance, promptness, politeness, and prayer. Next plant three rows of squash: squash gossip, squash criticism, squash indifference. Then add five rows of lettuce: let us love one another, let us be truthful, let us be faithful, let us be unselfish, let us be loyal. No garden can be complete without turnips: turn up for church, turn up with a smile, turn up a new idea, turn up with real determination!

Now that sounds like a challenging garden to plant. But maybe I should try one of those three squash varieties—then I won't have to worry about how we'll eat them. I think I'll have to plant patience in my pea rows.

The old-timers say all danger of damaging frost around here is past by the twenty-fourth of May, so that's the time to plant the impatiens in their beds. I saved two plants one fall with no hope of them surviving until spring. My house impatiens always end up being tossed out, as they get lice-infested. Well, surprise, surprise! Their blooms cheered us up all winter, and in March I took cuttings; I had my own impatiens to plant.

• • •

Another year, new items on my seed order were chives, endive, and everbearing strawberries. Chives are an herb from my childhood, growing beside the old bank barn. I also tacked on my order ten everbearing strawberry plants in addition to my regular strawberry plants to see what we think of late strawberries. Or will we have too many other fresh fruits by then and not even look at our strawberries?

I had never tried endive. Is there a reason many people aren't familiar with it?

Spinach was definitely a hit from my "plant new items" experiment one year. The baby spinach variety I grew made delicious salad. We ate it instead of lettuce. We also enjoyed a greens mixture that's ready first thing in the spring, along with the leaf lettuce. Only it is more interesting, with more flavor and vitamins, than leaf lettuce.

• • •

How did I manage to mess up such an ordinary, not-much-going-on Monday? I threw too many irons in the fire, I guess.

It was drizzling and chilly, but since it was a Monday it was laundry day. After lunch I decided that since the Pioneer Maid was crackling merrily I might as well haul up some of the tomato juice I had canned during busy September. I started with a half a batch of Farm Wife Lena's Marinara Sauce. Since that barely made a dent in the quarts of tomato juice, I continued with ketchup. First it was one batch, then two. May as well fill up a cooker with the third batch, I decided, then I'll be done with it. By that time the stove top was covered with pots, the countertops with jars, and Alyssa was busily stirring cookie dough.

After a few trips to serve shoe store customers, baking cookies, bottling sauce, and bringing laundry in, out of the drizzle, suppertime was here. By the time Allan came home from work all he could do was raise his brows and say, "What would you ever have done in your little house?"

We had recently changed houses with the Doddys so that we would have more room. And yet, every inch of my spacious countertop was covered with jars, kettles, sauce, canning dishes, cooking dishes, and baking dishes. Did it just take one month to forget how to clean up as you go so that you have room to work? Does more space just mean more mess?

Anyway, we ate our supper, the children went out with Dad, and I rallied the last of my energy. After I had bottled my ketchup, washed dishes, and wiped my spacious countertops, I was thankful for all my filled jars. I resolved to only tackle small bites the next day. One day of biting off more than I could chew was enough.

• • •

While I was cleaning our house for church here, the pickles grew to cucumbers, the place where I get peaches started taking orders, the beans grew long and fat, and the corn ripened. Forget about my thought of relaxing after hosting church.

As I can fruits and vegetables, I think I must look just like my mother. It all seems the same. Same smells of pickles, tomatoes, and fruit. I squint my eyes against the strong fumes of vinegar brine, just the way she did. The big dipper makes dull clunking sounds as it hits the jar funnel, same as hers. Only it wasn't my mother doing these big jobs. It was me, just the way I had always dreamed of when I was young. The big, big jobs were always much more appealing than my own. Canning is one job that is just as fun as it looked.

Canning with little ones is a challenge, though. I would stick baby Kyle wherever I had a chance to set him. He would soon grumble for greener pastures. He began his "crawling" in that season, managing to slip along the floor a few inches if he wanted something badly enough.

• • •

Fall is the time of year for picture-perfect basements in our community. The shelves are beautifully loaded with jars of gold, auburn, shades of green, cherry, orange, and ruby red. The potato bin is heaped with dull-red orbs. The carrots sleep beneath their layers of newspaper. Cabbages are piled crisp and green. The onions hang in their mesh bag. Beside them, the wood is piled in neat rows, with the chips swept away. Oh, beautiful!

• • •

In Grandma Albrecht's personal cookbook—old yellowed clippings from a local newspaper—readers discussed how to can peas. Busy housewives were looking for an alternative to steaming them for three hours. It suggested boiling one pint water, a half cup salt, and one cup sugar for five minutes. Add ten cups peas or fifteen cups of beans. Boil for ten minutes and put in hot, sterilized jars, and seal. They will not lose their color. To use, rinse them in cold water, bring to a full boil, and you have peas that taste and look fresh from the garden.

Another lady suggested: Take as many peas as you need and boil as long as you would for a meal. Have your jars ready, and also a kettle of boiling water. Dip your peas out and fill jars. If you don't have enough water from the peas, fill with the boiling water from the kettle. Add a half teaspoon salt in each jar, seal, invert, and leave till the next day. If there is no leakage, store away. When wanted for use, open jar, drain, and put peas in boiling water for five minutes. Drain and serve.

I never heard of those methods before. They intrigue me, although I really don't need them, as I freeze most of my peas. Those I don't are quickly sealed with my pressure canner.

Now, I wonder, how well would a discussion on canning peas go in today's daily newspaper?

A correspondent from Kentucky wrote, "Each year we plant peas hoping for a little to eat. Peas are a cool weather crop and don't do well here. Occasionally, I buy a bag of peas at the store. Those are soon licked up, and then we don't eat peas for a long, long time."

Hmm. I planted my garden later than most, so during the first week in July I've only just started to pick peas. Some ambitious gardeners plant their peas in March, during a mild spell, then let late snowfalls cover the seeds. So would Kentucky folks be okay if they planted their peas in January?

30

Then Comes Spring

IN SPRING THE BUZZ SAW whines a shrill tune most evenings as Allan cuts next winter's supply of shop firewood. As a new bride, I stared helplessly at that rippling blade, the wood chips, and the sawdust. I cringed at the noise of the old saw left from his grandfather's days. Everyone else helping looked comfortable and as if they knew their business. I learned quickly, if not willingly. There's a lot of wood to cut when you have two house stoves and two shop stoves. Especially if you live in Canada where the north winds blow cold.

With our little ones now, I no longer help with the wood very often. It looks as if we'll soon have more help. Eric shows signs of having inherited the love for wood from the line of Jantzi men before him. He'll sit and listen to the saw's whine and watch it's ripping teeth. When it's time to carry the wood away, he's right there. He examines each piece to find the cut end. With eyes twinkling, he shows everyone that here is where Dad cut the wood.

One morning, after a late night of cutting wood, he yawned and stretched. "Dad has to cut more wood," he announced. He's picking up his heritage lessons at a young age.

• • •

When I was a child, each spring Mommy Kuepfer would come bearing little packets of seeds. There was one for each of us children. They were labeled Kiddie Packets, and were packaged by the seed companies for twenty-five cents each. All kinds of interesting things grew from them. Strange varieties of beans, peas, and pumpkins, many pretty flowers, popcorn, and Swiss chard, to name a few.

We children spent hours sorting our seeds, and then Mom gave us part of a garden row to plant them in. They always grew like a jungle, planted too thickly by inexperienced hands.

After Alyssa and Eric joined our family, I was flipping through a seed catalog one spring and I spied them. Kiddie Packets, the ad announced, seventy-five cents each. I couldn't resist. I ordered two. My little ones sorted their seeds and planted a jungle.

The first thing peeking up in Eric's garden was a radish. He admired the sprout thoroughly, then promptly plucked it from its bed. "Is this a radish, Mom?" he asked.

Allan helped plant the potatoes one Saturday afternoon. I thanked him heartily for saving me a full day of work. He looked doubtful about it taking me a full day, but I told him to try it: take three children and a dog and plant four and a half long rows of potatoes. By suppertime you should be done.

• • •

I saved an old canning jar from Mommy Jantzi's collection. I was thinking it would look pretty filled with glass marbles, propping up my cookbook collection. Instead it became the caterpillar's home. Not a pretty caterpillar, just a common one. The kind that builds ugly web nests on tree branches. But it's a delight in our house. Whenever it crawls around its tiny home the children shout, "It's caterpillaring around!"

• • •

My interest was piqued by the haskap honeysuckle bush. Would the berries do well in our climate? Would they really almost taste like blueberries? Two varieties, borealis and berry blue, were sold as a package deal to ensure proper pollination. The instructions said that an even amount of moisture is essential for the first year. We planted them on the north side of the shanty beside the barn. When I feed our chickens, the berries get the leftover water. So far they're thriving on leftovers.

• • •

Before Alyssa drops off to sleep there's always some important question to get off her mind. One day it was, "Do bears have meat?" Before going to sleep at naptime she asked, "I never had an airplane ride. When are you going to take me on one?" One night she noted, "Horses and buggies go past in the middle of the night. Why, Mom?"

No wonder it takes her awhile to settle down to sleep with all that running through her mind.

• • •

Thoughts of springtime are always followed by dreams of my garden. In my mind I dream it will be our special spot where my little ones will eagerly join their mother. Baby will love digging in the earth at the end of the row. His happy siblings and mom will carefully drop the seeds in arrow-straight rows. The soft breezes will blow and the sun gently shine as we pat the soil over each tiny seed.

That's the dream. The end of April and beginning of May each year is when reality steps in. Everyone is eager to help. Too eager. Little hands reach for seeds only mothers plant. Baby protests his station with loud wails. His brother gleefully pulls up the row marker and digs a hole. Big sister watches soil sift through her fingers in favor of planting onion bulbs. My pocket bulges. It keeps my seed packages safe, plus all the empty bags stuffed on top.

Finally we trudge to the house, exhausted. The garden rows are partially planted. Everyone is dirty and hungry. By now my pocket is an unmanageable lump of full and empty packages and salvaged row markers, with soil sifting between it all.

What to do? I was loath to repeat the scene. My help came in a funny way. I was about to toss out my worn-out tie apron, when inspiration seized. Taking the full-length apron over to the sewing machine, I folded it up partway. I made three pockets by sewing along the sides and twice through the middle. One is for seeds to plant, the middle one for partially filled seed packets, and one for empty bags. With this apron tied around my middle, my tiny seeds are safe. And there is no unhandy bulge in my pocket. All I need is a water bottle and some snacks when I pack the little red wagon. Then we're off to live our dreams!

It really was that simple apron that saved my daydream, though. Without all those tiny seed packets to keep track of, I was less flustered. Being less flustered makes me more patient.

Patient moms have happy children. And happy children are really what makes the dream come true.

• • •

Simple fare tastes wonderful with warm breezes blowing through the open window. Especially to five-year-old Eric, who was sure that summer would never come.

"One day summer was going to come," he explained to a customer, "but then it got chilly and it went away again."

All things summer caught his eye. "Wouldn't that be nice if you wouldn't have to buy peanuts, Mom? I could grow some for you," he said, tugging me over to the grocery store's seed rack. He clutched the packet all the way home, dreaming aloud of heaps of peanuts. The back of the package taught us that peanuts can be grown in sandy soil in most parts of Canada. The one hundred growing days worried us, so Allan brought Jiffy-pots home to start them indoors. They did not like the house—just shriveled away as a potato would if you started it in the house, I suppose. We're northern gardeners, so we didn't know. October would show what happened to Eric's peanut dreams.

Our garden plot looks able to feed a dozen. I was idly wondering what to grow in all that space. A friend from Pennsylvania wrote, "Doesn't your horse need a meadow?" It does, but after the hard work of cleaning, leveling, and plowing, the plot holds a touch of sentiment. Grass seed isn't what was intended for the fertile soil. Instead, I added popcorn, pumpkins, raspberries, more strawberries, and flowers to my seed list. The children will each have a spot to plant their Kiddie Packets.

We will have wider rows so that Mabel and the walking cultivator can easily pass through. Pleasure-filled summer days with a garden large enough to plant all you please!

• • •

All I saw was the eight-dollar price tag and the flimsy, plastic contraption it hung from. He saw the endless possibilities of a butterfly net and all it could catch: butterflies, frogs, bugs, and maybe even fish, if they weren't too big.

This vision, and the hope that his mama might relent, brought the familiar question each time we entered the hardware store: "Mom, may we please have a butterfly net?"

Dreams fulfilled are often not easily recognized, especially when they're blurred by the actual vision and the eight-dollar net still hanging on the shelf. Sometimes if we allow ourselves, we realize the dream has already come true.

It was potato-planting time. Dad was digging the holes, the children put a potato and Epsom salts in each hole, and I covered everything. White moths in the clover field beside us lured Eric from the potato rows.

"Dad," he begged, "can I have a butterfly net? There's one at the hardware store that I really, really want and Mom never buys it for me."

His dad kept digging, but his eyes began to twinkle and a slow grin spread.

"I'd like to tell you a story," he began. Everyone forgot the potatoes and the hot sun and ran over to catch each word. "When I was a boy your size, our neighbors had a thrift store. Each year, they would also have a large garage sale. That year at the garage sale, I spied a small net. The price tag read one dollar. I knew that was a lot of money, but I set my heart on the net and raced home. How afraid I was that someone else would buy it before I got back! I begged and begged before my dad slowly reached into his pocket for a loonie dollar coin. I rushed back. How relieved I was to see the precious net still waiting for me!"

The children laughed and sighed with relief.

"To say the truth," their dad finished his story, "I don't remember ever using that net. I'm sure it's still around here. Let's get these potatoes in and we'll go look."

The potatoes were planted with gusto and everyone was off, leaving me to my covering job. By the time I finished, a smiling boy appeared. The net he carried was perfect for a four-year-old to catch butterflies, frogs, and fish. For a while, no butterfly in our yard escaped a chase with the net, and the drainage ditch was dragged for fish. Doddy's dollar was not lost after all. But dreams die hard. One afternoon at the hardware store, Eric began, "Mom, can I have—" before ducking his head in embarrassment. "Oh, I have one already!" he exclaimed.

• • •

We love to take our big, easy-rolling wagon when we go for a walk in summer. Alyssa walks beside Mom and Dad and the boys ride. I mean, Kyle patiently rides, and Eric frequently calls, "Whoa, whoa! There's a flower I could pick." Off he hops into the ditch or field to pick the beautiful wildflower blooms.

One day he triumphantly presented me with a handful of blooms. "Here, Mom," he said. "They're for Father's Day. I'm going to pick a whole case full." I suspected he meant something other than case. Soon my hands were overflowing—just like the vase when we reached home.

By the next morning the pretty bouquet was a sorry sight. Drooping flowers hung in all directions. Eric studied it carefully before deciding, "Our *case* doesn't look very good, does it Mom? Here, let me put fresh water in."

31

Wistful June

ONE YEAR I WAS UPSET about all the potato bugs we had. It seemed as if every last bug in Perth County paid a visit to my potato patch. And after I had chased Allan out in the rain to plant them I couldn't just let the bugs mow my patch down. So I picked the bugs. Each day I walked those rows. Sometimes twice a day I plucked the bugs from their leafy perches. Even Alyssa learned to pick potato bugs. I think we must have picked a four-liter coffee can full of them. But I wasn't upset anymore. We had the tallest, bushiest plants you ever saw, with the biggest red skin potatoes underneath.

For anyone not familiar with these beetles, the adults have hard-shelled wings striped in various browns and oranges. The babies hatch from soft, orange eggs located on the underside of the plants. They are soft, ugly, orange blobs that eat a mile a minute, and then suddenly there they are all grown up with shiny, new hard-shelled wings.

This latter part always intrigued me. Then one day, when I was in a better frame of mind, I had the opportunity to watch nature spin its web. While digging for our supper, there in the ground was an orange baby bug. Observing closely, I could see transparent wings forming. I'm sure, left undisturbed for a few days, it would have emerged from its dark hideout with a brand-new suit.

This year the gardens are a picture. They have had just a perfect mix of sun and rain. Now I just need to remember to lift my eyes from the gift to the Giver.

• • •

When I taught school, June was such a wistful month for me. I would pensively dismiss classes, then lock the school door one last time. Then I'd long to fit in with normal life.

Most times June would find me at Frey's berry patch, where there were acres and acres of strawberries waiting to be picked. We would start at the crack of dawn, crawling over the wet straw and hunting through the dewy plants. We'd pick until the hot sun had dried our wet clothes and sweat was dripping. Then we'd pick some more.

At night when we closed our eyes to rest, we saw acres and acres of berry plants swaying in the breeze. But we all learned perseverance, to anticipate Grandma Ada's scrumptious meals, and to make and drink strawberry juice. You fill your jar one-half to two-thirds full of washed, stemmed strawberries. Add sugar to taste, fill your jar with water, and shake. Hot-pack and process for ten minutes, and you have strawberry juice for the winter. Our children like it straight, but adding ginger ale when you open a canning jar to serve the juice really dresses it up.

These days, June isn't wistful, but it's still about strawberries. There are peas now too, and wispy sun-kissed children. It's long, long evenings outside and mornings that come too soon.

• • •

In June we love our outdoorsy washhouse with the warm breeze flowing through and the sun shining in. We completely forget the frozen fingers and toes of winter as we pitch all the heavy coats and blankets into the swirling waters. The children watch the activity from their mini lawn chairs as they eat their late breakfast. Soon they're begging for their own wash line, clothespins, and washcloths.

We've finally made them a wash line that works. It's simply bright blue baler twine threaded over insulators on T-fence stakes. Perfect, but hardly fashionable. It's easily rolled up and stored in the garden shanty for next washday, though.

It's the time of year to walk to the river to see mallard duck fathers frantically guard their families while the swallows swoop and dive. Once again Mother Canada Goose reigns on her nest at the top of the high, high hill—the hill made by humans that the train would climb before crossing the bridge running over the top of the road.

The daylight hours grow long and longer until there's never enough sleep. It's the time of living life to the fullest.

32

Preserving Summer's Bounty

WHEN I CLEAN MY FLOWER BEDS each fall there are always a few perfect geraniums, coleus, and impatiens begging to be potted and set in warmer temperatures. I always oblige, although I know their fate. They will die; I even know why they do.

Wouldn't you if you seldom got a drink? When you are at your thirstiest and beginning to shrivel you get a good drench. There, that will have to do for a long time until your next drenching. Finally, you have enough. You're withering again, and after your drench you continue to shrivel until you're pitched on the compost heap.

It happens every year, so I vowed I would not bring flowers in anymore. I'd skip the fuss and cut straight to the compost heap.

No such luck last fall. Alyssa and Eric arrived on the scene with a large stack of pots and rescued every pretty plant in the flower beds. After our pots were full they dug into Mommy Over There's collection.

All our plants were placed in the washhouse until we knew which ones would survive. Those were set on the living room and back room windowsills. Once or twice a week the children carefully gave them a little water. It looked hopeful that we'd have some left to replant after the May 24 frost date.

• • •

In the kitchen it's the most flavorful month as we cook the rosy mounds of tomatoes into pizza sauce, salsa, juice, and soup, or can them as chunk tomatoes. I acquired the best salsa recipe from sister Kathryn. She's the cook who doesn't measure or follow recipes very closely. But I did, and the salsa is delicious no matter who makes it! (Look for it in the recipe section at the end of this book.)

• • •

We are busy reaping the fruits of the gift we longed and sighed for. For weeks, it was kept from reach, wrapped in deep, white layers of cold. Next we wished to quickly tear away the layers of chilly, soggy days. Occasionally, when we despaired of ever enjoying the gift, bright sunshine from blue skies filled us with hope enough to carry us through the last cold, gray layers.

Those last layers were gradually stripped away by warm breezes and sunshine. Daffodils and tulips bloomed. Toes bared and leaves unfurled. There are barbecues and picnics, scooters and Rollerblades. Happiness reigns as we sing praises to God for this gift we've so graciously been given. Summer.

PART VII

It Takes a Community

33

Taking Care of Our Own

OUR CHILDREN have an extra grandmother! She's jolly, smiley, and laughs a lot while she rocks away, just as an eighty-three-year-old grandma should. When Alyssa was just two years old, she quickly nicknamed her Mommy Cathy. Mommy Cathy lived in the yellow house across the road from us before she moved in with Doddy Jantzis'. Mommy Cathy apparently never grows tired of endless questions and stories. You just plead, "*Komm, komm*," and she'll trot over to inspect dollies, farm animals, the scribbles on a paper, or the pictures in a book.

• • •

Mommy Jantzi was the fill-in caregiver for stroke patient Joe N. for a few days. He had a wheelchair and he got a ride on a sling when it was bedtime. "He's old, old, old," Alyssa explained to anyone who cared to listen. Mommy Cathy just chuckled from her rocking chair. Maybe she didn't feel as old anymore. I suppose she might even feel young and spry as she crawled into bed.

Aunt Ann, who now lives with Aunt Marion and Uncle Tom, is older now and not so spry. So she doesn't play soccer, as she used to. But she still pores over her crossword puzzles and enjoys Uno games, coloring, and singing. And we all know what October 13 means. That is Ann's very own special day, and she has now celebrated more than forty birthdays.

Mommy Cathy often tells the story of her youngest son. When it became obvious that he was not developing like her other boys, she took him to a children's specialist. After a long assessment the doctor asked, "Mrs. Jantzi, did you ever hear of Down syndrome?" She had not. The doctor gave her a brief education and sent her home. Her son, who was much more severely challenged than Aunt Ann is, lived with them for twenty years and never had more to eat than his bottle of milk.

We've come a long way since those days, but God still sends these special children. Medical technology still cannot "cure" them, but educators have learned much about ways they do learn and develop. They have come to bless us, gentle us, humble us, and slow our pace.

• • •

Then one day Mommy Cathy rode away in an ambulance and was in the hospital for many weeks. Alyssa would say, "I can't wait till tomorrow 'cause Catherine's coming home."

It just wasn't that simple for Mommy Cathy anymore. She was diagnosed with leukemia and her legs gave up on her.

At that point she was almost eighty-five, so youth was not on her side.

• • •

It has been said, "The road is long that never turns again." Well, what of the road that turns too often? Does it straighten again? We certainly hoped so. The week had taken us through many a loop and hairpin curve.

It started on Wednesday morning soon after Doddy Jantzis' left for a wedding. There was a knock, which heralded the arrival of Mommy Cathy's family and the news that she had passed on. This didn't come as a surprise, as she had been in the hospital and a nursing home for almost seven weeks. But I definitely had not planned on being alone to confirm funeral arrangements and oversee the neighbors who came to our aid! Since none of Mommy Cathy's family belonged to the Old Order Amish group, we hosted the funeral and viewing, which we were happy to do.

After the funeral on Saturday, Sunday hardly provided enough time to catch our breath before Monday came, along with "moving day." While everything was upside down anyway, this was the time we had decided to move out of our small *Dawdy Haus*, meant for elders, and hand it over to the real Doddys. There was a lot to do to try to catch up and settle in. For weeks the children still begged to go "home," which was easy for them to do, as we just moved to the house next door. It never took long until they were back, though!

Mommy Cathy had lived with Doddy Jantzis' for over a year. I always thought that Mommy Jantzi's and my own caregiving duties were very similar. But on my side of the house the diapers were small and manageable. The childlike antics were cute and tears were rocked and kissed away. Mommy Jantzi's job— caring for an elderly woman—was not as easy.

Although Mommy Cathy was human like each of us, with some days better than others, she had such a jolly spirit. I knew that she had experienced more than a fair share of life's hard knocks, and so I often pondered this. Recently I read, "Some things it seems can only come through the gates of tribulation. Such traits as faith, hope, love, gentleness, and sympathy find no other way of entrance into our lives but by sorrow." I suppose these same tribulations could just as easily, or maybe more easily, cause a hard, bitter heart.

• • •

Doddy Over There had been recovering well from his quadruple bypass heart surgery. The children ran next door when it was his exercise time. They were quick to show how easy it is to reach for the sky and do their favorite exercise: breathe in, breathe out, and cough.

34

Love in the Air:
An Amish Wedding

JUNE IS THE MONTH so many of our Amish young people choose for their wedding day. Of course everyone can't use the same month, so the weddings here start in the spring and drag into the fall. The "wedding of the year" (well, for our family, at least) is already history. I'd like to tell you all about my sister's big day and the days leading up to it.

A week and a half before the special day, Susan Albrecht and Paul Zehr's intentions were publicly announced by the bishop after church services, even though the family had privately been preparing for weeks. During the week after the Sunday announcement, their neighbors and friends watched eagerly for the *hochzeiters*, or engaged couple. A visit from the bride- and groom-to-be is a sure way of gathering a family together. Everyone is eager to hear the groom formally invite them and tell them where the service will be held. Invitations are mailed to those who live too far off to invite personally.

We cleaned out Dad's shop and set up three lengths of tables. The living room was also cleared for the *eck* (corner) table. A beautiful white wedding cake and side cakes Susan decorated would go on this table, with bouquets of white and purple roses and white lilies. Hurricane candleholders with grapevine finished out the "wings" of this table.

The Monday before the wedding we cut up all the bread for the dressing.

Tuesday we mixed the Jell-O salad, which was orange flavored with carrots and a sprinkle of celery. The tables were set and the cooking pots made ready for morning.

No prodding to get out of bed was needed the big morning of Wednesday, March 31. This was the first wedding my parents hosted since my own almost four years earlier. I was determined not to miss a minute of it! I must have acquired some organizing skills since my wedding, as we managed to dress ourselves, plus the two babies, and pull into the yard just as my parents finished frying the last batch of chicken legs and thighs.

My sister and her two attendants (who were my other sisters!) were neatly dressed in their black dresses and white nylon capes and aprons. The buggies glistened in the early morning sun as they left for the wedding service at neighbor Lorne Kuepfers'.

Meanwhile, the cooks arrived. The old-fashioned black iron kettle stove was fired up to make the large batches of dressing. The older women were the dressing cooks. They fried onions and celery in butter. Then the bread was added, then the seasonings, an egg-and-milk mixture, and chicken broth. By this time, the men were stirring and the women bossing.

Large kettles of long-grain rice were set to cook. Each woman added salt, seasoning, and chicken broth to taste, and stirred and stirred her pot of rice to perfection.

In the washhouse, we set the stainless steel bake ovens on top of Coleman camp stoves. We rolled more chicken pieces in a shake-and-bake mix from a bulk foods store, then oven-fried them in butter.

More cooks were preparing the broccoli and cauliflower salad. The table waiters cut the marble and carrot cakes and the chocolate and pecan pies. They dished out the fruit salad and set out pickles, salads, applesauce, rolls, butter, ham, and bologna.

Soon all was ready, and the cooks and table waiters ate buffet style before leaving for the service. After observing the uniting of the bride and groom, we hurried back to put the finishing touches on the meal.

After everyone was seated to eat, Paul's nephews and friends of the bride ate with them at the *eck* table. Six girls were chosen to serve this special table.

Paul's sister-in-law and I passed around the traditional wedding fruitcake. This cake had been cut and wrapped beforehand, and the cakes in the corner remained untouched.

When the meal was completed, the men and women gathered to sing the usual German wedding hymns. The start of this singing was the signal to three little girls to carry the wine bottles to the groom. Each returned, smiling happily, with the gift they received for doing their duty.

The groom then filled tiny glasses with a sip of wine, which corner servers passed to the guests. As the wine bottles emptied, the groom's mother refilled them until each guest received a glass, in remembrance of how Jesus once turned water into wine at a wedding.

After the singing, the bishop met with the newlyweds and witnesses to sign the marriage certificate. The guests gathered their gifts to present to the couple waiting in an upstairs room. Meanwhile, the wedding attendants passed out candy and peanuts.

Later in the day, a leftover supper was served on a first-come, first-served basis. More hymns were sung, and last of all the "Ehestund Lied" ("Marriage Song").

Before you know it, all that remained of the day was pleasant memories!

• • •

My children didn't know what a wedding was. It had been two and a half years since we attended one. May would change that. Aunt Laura, my youngest sister, had her special day planned for the twenty-second. So there was a new light purple dress, nylon apron, and cap to admire. Discussing the big day had no end. Explanations and instructions on their special jobs were practiced and repeated. Then they whispered of the gifts they were sure to receive after a good performance.

This probably gave them a twisted view of weddings. Next time there will be no new clothes or special jobs or gifts. It will be different when it's not an aunt's wedding. Except for the food. There will always be the unique Milverton Amish–style dressing and rice, with the meat being chicken and cold cuts. Salads usually include the traditional salad made with orange Jell-O and shredded carrots. Dessert includes pies, cakes, and fruit salad. But not all Old Order Amish weddings serve wine, as we do in our community.

• • •

We eagerly left early to help sister Laura move after her wedding. What fun, washing all the shiny new dishes and trying to fit her things into tight corners to create a cozy little home for two. Of course, it seems like yesterday that my sisters were helping me. But it wasn't. Two multiplied to five by the time of Laura's wedding; how quickly we outgrew our first, cozy quarters. I sigh. To think how I forgot to fully enjoy those newlywed years. Being young, I was always ready and pushing for the next step of life, forgetting to savor the moment that is. I'm still young, so maybe I still don't appreciate time as I should, but I'm getting better at it. I think of the poem by Canadian poet Frederick George Scott that I used to read to my students during literature class, which roughly goes like this: "Why hurry to the sea? / There is nothing there to do / but sink into the blue. / . . . In the tides forever more / on that far-off, distant shore . . ."

35

Our Amish Benefit Auction

AS INEVITABLE AS SUMMER is to July, so is the Milverton Amish school sale.

Around the time that the schools close their doors for the term, you'll begin to notice small advertisements in newspapers or large ones hanging in local shops and businesses. All of these advertisements urge you to attend the next annual consignment auction, which is held for the Milverton Area Amish School Fund. Many local people, the Amish community, and tourists come. Most go year after year. Approximately eight thousand to ten thousand attend.

If you visit, surely one of the five to six auction rings will be offering something that interests you. Perhaps you're looking for a new horse to pull the family carriage. Here you have a good choice of around two hundred horses or ponies. Maybe it was a carriage you wanted. You'll find that too. One hundred quilts, various antiques, machinery, household items, and even pets will be auctioned as well.

If the auctioneers' chants don't excite you, perhaps you'll be interested in a snack from the food booth. After all, someone has to buy the approximately 190 dozen hamburgers, 210 dozen sausages on a bun, 100 dozen hot dogs, 405 cases of pop, 3,000 bottles of water, and 2,000 ice cream cones—plus other items. You can also head over to the busy bake sale.

The day before the sale, the ladies worked hard preparing 700 pies and other baked goods. The morning of the sale, a few early birds fried 240 dozen doughnuts.

Local businesses also bring their wares and set up shop. One man was even making ice cream with an ice cream maker powered by a John Deere motor.

Over in the large machinery shed you'll find another group of busy people. They're the ones who deal with the financial part of the sale, preparing bills and collecting payment for the items you buy. For some of these people, the work continues for many days after the sale.

A committee of four men has been appointed to ensure that everything runs smoothly. Others have been assigned to take care of consigning items, and organizing horse and quilt sales, the food booth, the bake sale, and the office. Many people spend many hours to make this sale successful each year. If you'd like to host the sale, you'll need between thirty and thirty-five acres of grassland.

The sale has been held each summer for twenty years. Who planned and organized the first one?

Like most ideas, it all started with one person—in this case, my father, Eldon Albrecht—and was made a success by many.

My mother wrote in her diary: "After reading of all the successful money-raising school sales in the *Budget*, Eldon also got this in his head. 'Let's make one here this summer,' he announced one evening. The children went wild."

Mom, thinking of all the work it could be, said "No way!" The children either never heard or were too full of their own dreams of what such a day would bring.

After many decisions and much planning, sheets were sent out to the community asking for a list of the items they had to sell. When the lists slowly trickled in, my parents were disappointed with the number of items. "Make it anyway," some people encouraged. "More things will come."

So with the help of Bill Horst, the local auctioneer, Dad got a sale flier together. Mom wrote: "Surprise! People are alarmed at all the goodies for sale; horses, pets, machinery, and household items."

The first sale date was set for July 20, 1996, thanks to the encouragement of some and despite the discouragement and pessimistic views of many others. Because my parents were very busy when the items started arriving for the sale, my brother and I, ages twelve and eleven, respectively, were responsible for numbering and recording each consigned item! No wonder there were problems for the bookkeepers after the sale!

We filled up the orchard and a small field with machinery and the front lawn with household items. The quilts were all draped over a clotheshorse and the thirteen horses were led from our barn to the driveway to be sold. Mom set up a food booth in Dad's metal shop where the ladies sold 40 cases of pop, 300 cups of coffee, 40 dozen hamburgers, 40 dozen hot dogs, and 600 ice cream cones, plus other items.

A few neighbor girls set up the office on a card table. They soon ran out of space and shoved together some benches to make another makeshift table. When the memorable day was over, my parents were well satisfied. The sale had been well attended and bidding had been brisk.

Already our neighbors were making plans to be the hosts for next year's sale.

For many evenings afterward the "office girls" returned to help my parents with the bookwork. When they had everything semi-straightened out, they were left with over $6,000 to donate to the schools, proving that it had been a successful first sale! It is still going strong.

36

Generous Hands

SISTER KATHRYN HAD TRAVELING PLANS. She was going with a group of single girls and David and Esther to Texas. Hopefully we would survive until her return two weeks later.

It's the little details that are so amazing. God knew to scatter singles, such as my sister, and couples with no children among busy, growing families. God knew we would need these special people with generous hands; hands to take our babies when our arms are full. They wash more than their share of dishes at gatherings. They care for our elderly. Teach our schools. They babysit our little ones and help us get our homes in order for church services. They bring meals to those who need them and write letters. They keep their sewing machines busy. Busy hands scattering blessings. I think each of us has our own story of how these many hands have benefited us.

I wished the travelers a great trip. Might they come home feeling rejuvenated, with sleeves rolled up ready to go at it again.

• • •

I can't help but think that life is so unfair. I sat one day at church surrounded by my healthy family. Beside me was a young mother who had just buried her six-month-old daughter; off to the side was another mother and her young daughter whose daddy was battling multiple sclerosis. There sat my cousin with empty arms and a husband with major heart problems. The burdens seemed so heavy, and who else was struggling that I knew nothing of? But we were reminded that the Lord will not give us more than he will help us carry. He keeps his promises. See the rainbow. We see but dimly as through a glass. Would life still seem unfair if we could see more clearly that these trials lead to heaven?

Many, through unbelief, ignorance, or life's circumstances, must bear their burdens alone. We have a precious heritage and faith.

37

Off to School

As SEPTEMBER SCHOOL DAYS NEAR, the golden days and cool nights set my teacher's heart astir. I can just hear my students chanting their memory verses from James Whitcomb Riley: "When the frost is on the pumpkin and the moon is yellow cheese . . ."

The first memory piece of a new school term is no problem for students to memorize. The school still smells of fresh paint and varnish. The books are clean and crisp and the pencils long and sharp. Enthusiasm is high! The students can gather seeds, catch insects or spiders, or maybe even dig up an anthill. That all depends on what we're studying for science. Learning is fun and hands-on this time of year and you're sure you'll teach forever.

September does have one fault, though. It throws too many broad hints that summer is over and winter is just around the corner. Oh well, the allergy sufferers will have no problem with that.

One Sunday I sniffed, sneezed, and snuffled my way through services. Just after I had every Kleenex in my pocket thoroughly soaked, little Eric started up. He was sneezing mini atchoo-atchoos, tears streaming down his cheeks and his nose running. He just couldn't stop! Atchoo, atchoo, and oh—ah—tchoo! Welcome to the family, Eric! Isn't it amazing what we pass on to our children? But hay fever when you're six months old?

I just finished reading an article on dishwashing. Train your children to be good dishwashers and you'll make a good first grader, they say. Oh, I most certainly want that! But what? They want me to start training at two years of age? You mean I have to give up my nice, warm sinkful of sudsy water and my scalding-hot rinse water? It takes but a few pleasant swishes, and my small stack of dishes are sparkling clean. Now I have to give that up? But I do want a good first grader. Broken dishes shouldn't concern me too much. I must have been on "a dish a day" spree myself. I even broke the beloved coffeepot sister Susan so unselfishly gave from her cupboard. All that remains is the plastic cone that holds the filter. I'm sad about that one.

One Saturday afternoon while cleaning, neighbor Lindsay broke a water glass. After giving himself a thorough scolding, he moaned, "And that's already the second dish I broke since Allie died." His wife had only been gone for nine years. He could teach me a few things about being careful.

"Ah, tough," were the words coming from the kitchen while I was in the bathroom. It turned out Alyssa was having a "tough" time folding Mom's glasses. Maybe that's because they were being folded backward? It reminded me of the little skit we had at one of our Christmas concerts. The little boy tells Mom that he lost his glasses, and they both go hunt for them. The little boy soon gives up, but Mom hunts and hunts. When he inquires why she keeps hunting in vain she replies, "You're searching for a pair of glasses and I'm looking for two hundred and fifty dollars."

So here I was, in the city needing glasses, searching for something half decent for an Amish lady to wear. Each pair seemed more bold and more square, and the temples thicker. Now everywhere I go people notice my new glasses! It must be because silver, rectangular specs don't exactly complement a long, narrow face. Alyssa is quite lavish with her compliments!

They say you can't teach an old dog new tricks. Well, I'm determined to prove them wrong again. It all started when Eric came along and I needed a hand with the shoe store customers, especially as business picked up each September. Mommy Jantzi was the most obvious candidate. So we learned all about Ontario's tax requirements. Charge GST (general sales tax 5 percent) on everything. Charge PST (provincial sales tax 8 percent) on all footwear over thirty dollars, plus all other goods except children's clothing. Besides all that, she learned to run the calculator after sixty-six years of just using her head. Just when things were running well and we were congratulating ourselves for proving the old saying wrong, along comes HST (harmonized sales tax). The government combined GST with PST to create a single 13-percent HST. So here we go again . . .

When the frost is on the pumpkin . . .

• • •

I knew I'd feel excited. Of course, new experiences always cause excitement, even if it means sending your oldest child to school. Alyssa was invited to her first day of kindergarten. I also expected to feel a little anxious. Who doesn't when you're experiencing something new? The overwhelming gratefulness I felt was normal, I thought, with all we had to be thankful for. There were her friends that took her to school, a Christian school and teacher, and living in a country that allows this to happen. The list is endless, really.

In the end I even had to admit to a little sadness. Just a pinch when I realized my baby was spreading her wings and flying from my constant care. Those, however, were not the feelings that threatened to overwhelm me on that day and made the time so long. It was loneliness. I never knew how lonely my kitchen would feel void of her constant chattering. There was no loud supervising of her brothers, no begging to do the things too big, no whining when she was bored, no clatter of her dishwashing, no flower watering, no sink scrubbing, or floor sweeping.

The questions were gone too. What does this word say? Would you please read me this book? Can you help me with my next preschool workbook page?

When the boys were napping I even felt the loneliness in my easy chair. There was no wiggle-worm beside me reading her own story or writing her own letter. No one was constantly interrupting my quiet time with questions or insisting I look at her interesting pictures.

I never expected the longing that would seize me at 4:00 p.m. Nor how anxiously I would watch the road until suddenly there she was with her lunch pail and her papers and ready to tell me all about her day! What a wonderful day it was!

First she rode to school on the neighbor children's coveted pony cart. When she got there, (wonder of wonders!) there was a desk with a piece of tape on it and on the tape was printed "Alyssa" and that is how she knew that that was her desk. All the other students said good morning to the teacher (but she forgot).

She listened to a Bible story of the children of Israel grumbling for water and Moses striking a rock to get some. After reciting the Lord's Prayer they sang some songs that she didn't always know the words to, but she tried to help as hard as she could.

After that she sat for a long, long time while all the other children got out books, pencils, and papers. Then at last the teacher said, "Kindergarten may come to the front," and that meant that she could walk to the teacher's desk. The teacher gave them a page of work—very easy work. Only she and two other children got to do that easy work. All the others had hard, hard work. So hard they sometimes had to put up their hand to ask the teacher how to do it.

And she always remembered to raise her hand before she talked. Even when the other kindergarten children were all talking without raising their hands, she still remembered to. Then was recess time when everyone could run outside and play. After that she did more work, listened to stories, and made a little yellow duck with wings, legs, and a head that could move.

Next it was time to eat the good bologna sandwich and play outside before the fall party that afternoon.

When they came in there were party games to play, punch to drink, and snacks to eat. Then everyone seemed to be getting ready to play outside again, but the teacher said they were getting ready to go home. She was glad, because she felt very tired.

That day whetted her appetite for more, and she eagerly waited for spring. Then she might go to kindergarten every second day.

• • •

Alyssa packed and repacked her bag, deciding what should and should not go along to school. Should she choose new shoes from the store? And just how many more days until school started, Mom? She had pinned her hopes and happiness to the little white schoolhouse a mile up the road. For the first time in her six years, she would be on her own. I remained behind to launder, clean, nourish, and most importantly, pray. Together we'll work to make her school years all she thinks they will be.

• • •

There are all sorts of things mothers do the day their first-born goes to actual school. I've heard of some that occasionally wipe tears with the corner of their apron as they make preparations. Some work hard to restrain themselves from gathering their young one in their arms and reassuring him that he may stay home awhile longer. Others just sit down and sob.

I felt slightly hardhearted as the big day approached and I felt none of the above emotions. I have to admit to feeling as elated as my daughter did as we filled her backpack, laid out new school clothes, and packed a lunch.

"We are back in the school system," I sang happily to my husband. "It makes me feel complete again."

And then came the day I filled the void that formed over six years earlier when I left the parochial system that had become so important to me. I had first entered the system as an eager first grader. Several years after my graduation, I entered as a novice teacher. The day Alyssa went to school, we started as inexperienced, young parents. We were ready to be part of the system that requires much labor from parents, students, and teachers.

"All teachers should first be parents. All parents should first be teachers." This was something I first heard while I was teaching school. "Probably," I decided uncertainly. Now that I'm a parent, I see the wisdom in those two lines. I can recall many teaching incidents that I would now handle differently, had I known what I know now. I have no doubt but that these incidents will increase as my children grow older.

Once at a teacher's meeting the paper from the question box read: "What should a grade-one student know before he comes to school?"

"Obedience," came the answer. "How adeptly we could teach if each student entered school perfectly obedient. Mothers should leave the teaching of academics to the teacher." I agreed to this answer, heartily, in my opinionated, schoolteacher way. I still agree with that teacher's answer, but it is no longer black-and-white.

As a teacher, I never considered how long an older preschool child's winter can be. As a mom, I began to rely on schoolwork to bring spring quickly. The winter was long and my daughter an eager student. Before warm breezes blew, she had learned more than what would please most first-grade teachers.

I also forgot that obedience is not taught in one, two, or even three lessons. It might be better compared to straightening crooked teeth with braces. Constant pressure does a better job than one quick, hard jerk. Eventually the braces must be removed, even if some of the teeth are not yet perfectly straight. In the same way, we free our children to go to school even with imperfections and flaws. We trust the teacher will help them grow and we'll continue our work at home. Too often, I see it's because of my own weaknesses that my children's growth is stunted.

This time we were doing it right by being teachers first before becoming parents. We realize, though, that there will still be lots of mistakes made and growing to do on our part.

Far too often things are not as they first appear. Early rising was no problem for Alyssa the morning she was traveling to Toronto. She was going shoe shopping for our store with her parents. There was no napping with the many sights on the busy highway. "They use that lumber to build elephant cages," she announced confidently, pointing to the lumber truck that roared past. By the time we had suppressed our laughter, our van had again passed the lumber truck. That's when we saw the row of elephants stamped on the lumber's wrapper. If you can't read, you could easily misinterpret the elephant pictures to mean "This lumber is used for building elephant cages."

Soon she will no longer make such mistakes. After coming home from her third day of school, she happily plopped on the couch. From the paper in her pocket she read, "John, John. Look, John. Look, Janet. John and Janet. Look, look!"

Eric danced around the kitchen crowing, "Alyssa can read! Alyssa can read!"

38

Holding Amish Church Services

THE TRADITION OF HELPING each other is a blessing of our community life. I felt warm and tingly as I crawled into bed. The walls and ceilings of our tiny house were free of their dust and cobwebs. The next day I smiled as I reminisced about the world's problems that we solved (though not many of our own), the news discussed, and topics of interest we shared. Precious heritage. We've been reminded that too many people appreciate their heritage but do nothing to preserve it. Lord, help me to remember that I'm never too busy to help get ready for church services at my house or others' homes.

As an added blessing, soon after sister Susan moved our chime mantel clock, it started to chime at the quarter hour. "Eek," I shrieked, "that clock hasn't chimed since the first years of our marriage!"

It's been doing its duty ever since. It chimes out each quarter hour, much to the delight of our children. I almost feel like a newlywed again!

• • •

When the decision is made to hold church services at our house, it gives us thoughts of neglected corners, chipped paint, and broken spindles. You put your thoughts to action. You want all your walls scrubbed, windows washed, ceilings freed of cobwebs, and cupboards cleaned and straightened. Suddenly your days are longer and fuller and you're ready for bed earlier, but because of all the extra tasks, you get there later. Out of the weariness, and probably the stress, by now you aren't a very pleasant person to live with. Dad and the children stay out of your way and heartily wish church were over with. That's when it's time to stop and think of this little story:

Down the road and around the corner from where we live is a little town named Milverton. Now, anyone familiar with Milverton also knows the name Guenther. You automatically connect it with your bread supply. As far back as I remember or my mother remembers, and even my grandmother remembers, you could count on a Guenther to bake your bread and deliver it too. Currently there are three Guenther men busily employed at the task. Several of my sisters have enjoyed helping with bakery duties. They also learned the Guenthers are men of few words, with those generally being very sufficient.

It was when my sister asked for a day off bakery duties to help clean for church that she received this answer; "Too much cleaning. Not enough praying."

• • •

Folks from the middle and west church districts gathered in our shop one winter to sort cast-off sheets from local motels.

The sheets would be given a second life in third-world countries after volunteers turned them into smaller sheets, comfort tops, or bandages. Cedar Grove Mennonite Church supplied us and took care of the end product.

Alyssa and Eric enjoyed all the extra attention from Allan's brother Sam and his wife, Edith, during this time. One morning the little ones were being especially sweet and cooperative and I burst out, "Oh, you sweet little things. What would Mom and Dad ever do without you?"

Alyssa looked over solemnly. "Sam would take us," she said.

"But then what would Mom and Dad do without our little ones?" I asked again.

Alyssa had an answer for that one too. "Sam said you'd buy more," she replied.

• • •

During a church service, a man led out the familiar "Loblied" with the faltering voice of a beginner. It was soon evident that he had not tried the role of song leader frequently. Bravely, he carried on although he didn't always find the correct pitch. Always there was someone experienced to put him back on the right track.

After the last strains of the aged song had faded, the visiting bishop rose. He mentioned that he saw the off-pitch music as a beautiful thing. It was a perfect example of a harmonious church. We must willingly help the erring one, and gently lead him back to the right track. Take him there again and again, and all pitch in and walk beside him. Forget that he sang the tune wrong before and let him try again.

And like the erring song leader, we must gladly accept help. Never stubbornly sticking to our own faltering tune, but joining those who've faithfully sung it for years.

39

Our Milverton Amish

IN OUR AREA we have large fields of grain, corn, hay, and soybeans. Besides the Amish, there are many hardworking Swiss and Dutch farmers settled here.

In our church district of twenty-five families there are only five full-time farmers. Two have cow herds and one has a goat herd. Two others farm pigs. Six do farming and also work away from home or have shops. The rest work in shops or at construction and a few are retired or semiretired. These days, farms are often bought in partnership or not at all, as more and more young people are just buying small lots.

Cow dairies are fading because of the huge start-up funds needed. This includes many dollars needed to buy your "quota," which gives you the privilege to ship milk. Goat and sheep dairies are gaining in popularity. The large Old Order Mennonite community east of here has organized a produce auction. It has been reasonably successful, probably because of the "buy local, buy fresh" movement that is sweeping the country. Our local grocer has been making twice-a-week trips to the auction for a few years now.

Most of our families have large kitchen gardens. Some have produce stands at the roadside and others sell to the organic market. As far as I know, little from here is trucked to the produce auction.

· · ·

There are a total of ten surnames currently being used in our community. The most common of these is Kuepfer.[1] These Kuepfers migrated from western Switzerland, and Andrew and Jacob Kuepfer are the ancestors of most of the Kuepfers in Ontario. In Canada, the spelling of this surname was changed to English. Some added an *e* (Kuepfer), and others used Kipfer.

The pronunciation of Albrecht, my maiden name, is a surprise to most. We all say "Albright" whether it applies or not! It is believed that we originated from Bavaria, Germany, from the family of Johannes and Barbara Albrecht.

The Jantzis can be traced back to Alsace-Lorraine, France. The name also causes pronunciation problems, as most people want to say "Jan-tzee" instead of using the German pronunciation, where the *J* gets a *y* sound.

The Streicher family also came from Bavaria, Germany.

Christian and Anne Maria Wagler are the ancestors of most Waglers in our community.

The Zehr family can be traced back to Switzerland. Joseph C. and Katherine (Yoder) Zehr came to Canada in 1860.

There are a handful of families here using the Schmidt last name. They originate from John Schmidt, who married Barbara Schwartzentruber of Lancaster County in 1831.

The Ebersols originated from Christian and Suzanna Ebersol, originally of Imling, France. All the Ebersols of this community

---

[1] I used information from *A Glimpse of Our Ancestors* for this chapter.

are children, grandchildren, or great-grandchildren of John K. Ebersol. His family of nine boys is keeping this surname alive in our community. Many of their relatives live in Pennsylvania. In October 2005, John was remarried to Amanda L. (Beiler) King of Pennsylvania.

Only two single women still sign their name Herrfort. This surname was buried with bachelor Andrew Herrfort this past spring. Andrew does have a brother, Solomon; Solomon and his family live in the United States.

Recently, twin brothers joined our church and married sisters. Both have families, thus adding Davidson to our list of surnames.

• • •

During the twentieth century, immigrants from the rest of the world changed our area permanently. Today its cities are home to some of the most multicultural places in the world. Over the years, waves of Jewish, Ukrainian, Italian, Portuguese, Asian, Jamaican, East Indian, and Somali immigrants have each added their own special contribution.

I have many opportunities to meet these immigrants or their descendants. Our family doctor trains those who are students in the medical profession. Also, a lot of shoe merchants and salespeople are from many other countries.

I always say we get fewer stares when we visit the big towns today. Everyone else is dressed differently too!

PART VIII

From the Jantzi Shoe Box

40

Songs and Customer Service

PEOPLE WERE THINKING about their feet again. It has been said that we don't think about our feet until they hurt (or get cold, I might add). When was the last time you bent over in the shower and gave your feet a good scrubbing? Do you even towel them dry, or just hope the air will do the trick? For something that we hope will carry us for about 185,150 kilometers—or 115,000 miles—in our lifetime, we sure manage to abuse them. But the cold and snow of our climate always force folks to think of their feet again. That means fall is the busiest season at our shoe store.

A new baby smack in the midst of the fall season one year caused some hectic days. Mommy Jantzi came to our rescue again, and also Mommy Albrecht and the aunts. It takes weakness to appreciate being the receiver. While recovering from birth is a joyful time, mothers still need time to heal and rest. And so we feel so grateful yet humbled by the many meals, gifts, helping hands, letters, and cards we receive. We hope to pass the kindness on someday.

• • •

We were ready to unwind after a busy three-day spring sale in the shoe store. Cousin Jolene came over with a packed lunch, so we added to it and headed to the river. There on its banks we ate our lunch to the music of red-winged blackbirds, orioles, and robins, the chirping of the cliff swallows, and the honking of geese. We discovered we were sitting above a muskrat's home, and followed his trail to the river. For a fleeting moment, Alyssa wished she could be a muskrat. That was until Jolene reminded her that she could get caught in a trap. Even the ants carrying the crumbs away were much more appealing than those at home on the countertop. We returned home tired and totally unwound.

• • •

Recently, I heard that between 10:00 a.m. and 2:00 p.m. is the ideal time to do things like ask your boss for a raise, ask others for special favors, and so on.

I guess I've been subconsciously following this bit of advice when calling in my shoe orders. Not too early, when the sales reps are still yawning and drinking their coffee. Not too late, or they are too wrapped up in ending their day and don't give your order priority. Yah, between ten and two sounds about right.

41

Too Many Shoes

WE SHOULD'VE LIVED in Grandfather's day. Then we'd each just have one pair of shoes, versus the four pairs our children have. I think they might even be happier with one pair. They prefer bare feet. That is a problem sometimes. You leave the house properly shod and come back in with bare toes and no idea where your shoes are. Rainy days come and go with no rubber boots in sight. Trips to town are preceded by frantic shoe searching.

But one week I was finding shoes instead of losing them. In our shoe store there's a little cubbyhole under the steps. It's the perfect hidey-hole for little tots. I was on my knees in the cubbyhole searching for other things when I found Eric's cache. It consisted of a pair of Dawgs (soft boots), his rubber boots, plus his sunglasses. He fared better than Alyssa. As I wrote in my *Connection* column, our helpful neighbor boys found her rubber boots baled into a hay bale! Tears rolled at the sight of the missing toe and the huge slashes on the boots.

We learned something here. One pair of footwear is sufficient. That's all that's around most of the time anyway!

· · ·

It was time to pull the winter boots from storage. Our farmer friend left his in the basement for the summer. When he pulled them on after their long rest, he found them much too tight. It felt as if the inside of the boot had swollen at the toe. Since the boots were almost new, he brought them back to the shop. I agreed that such a thing should not have happened, so I called the company about it. The voice at the other end of the line instructed me to take a picture of the problem with my phone, and send it to them. While explaining how impossible that would be for me to do, she cut me short. "You're one of those Mennonites, aren't you? Don't worry, I'll send you a credit slip and you can give the farmer a new pair of boots. Which size did you say they were?"

So we parted happily. The farmer with his new pair of boots and me with my hassle free credit slip.

Before Allan threw the discarded pair of boots into the furnace, he decided to have a closer look at the problem. With a little scraping and prodding, he successfully removed all the tightly packed manure, which had somehow fallen down in the boot around the toe. Now the boots were as good as new.

What now? I already had my credit slip and the new boots were already worn. It's a large company and one free pair of boots wouldn't hurt them. I couldn't forget the trust that saleslady had for those Mennonites, though. Integrity won. I tore up that slip.

Lest I ever feel proud of our honesty, I happened across a little story:

A man and woman went to a local chicken place and ordered two buckets of take-out chicken. After finding a quiet picnic spot beside a beautiful river, they proceeded to enjoy their chicken. Imagine their surprise to find one bucket filled with gold!

They promptly returned the bucket of gold and exchanged it for a chicken-filled one. The manager, impressed with the couple's integrity, sent out a reporter for the local news. After jotting down the details of the story, the reporter requested a picture of the couple.

To this the man firmly refused. "You see," he explained, "this woman is not my wife."

• • •

October brings a slowing of the pace, the finishing of tasks, the start of our shop work, and the free flow of shoe store customers. We welcome the change of pace and the comfortable feeling of winter still in the distance. We watch the children meet at the corner and then scooter past to school. I breathe a prayer wishing each student and teacher a happy, educational day. I wish for each to practice true integrity and the golden rule Jesus gave us to follow.

42

The Wadded Sock

ON COLD WINTER DAYS, I have to keep trotting from the kitchen stove to the basement stove and out to the furnace that heats the shop and store—to keep all the fires going. By spring the woodsmoke will have permanently saturated my clothes and skin, I'm afraid. Except for keeping the fires going, no one expects us anywhere. On stormy days, no one even comes to the store.

In the house it is pleasantly comfortable and, most of all, warm. I sew and the children content themselves by playing or watching the blowing snow and digging up warm memories. Eric recalled, "Remember that hot day when we were putting in wood and Mommy called, 'Watermelon'?"

It reminds me of our wood buried under the snowdrifts, and I wish more hot days had been spent storing it in the cellar.

When the winds die we thrive—as shoe store owners—on others' cold toes and fingers. The children are glad for the break and troop outside with me. They jump in the snow or, like little otters, slide down the banks. Our world looks like a scene from the Sahara Desert. We have wind-swirled drifts and banks of snow instead of sand. In our desert you would be more apt to freeze instead of perish from thirst. When the sun shines even the sky looks frozen, and the sun's rays only reach so far before they are intersected by brilliant sun dogs.

• • •

Recently I read an article that asked some thought-provoking questions: If we were to take a pen and write down these three words, Amish, Canadian (or American), and Christian, and then arrange these words in a sequence of our priorities, what order would they be in? Which order should we be?

The article related this to how the Mennonites in Germany during the Third Reich chose the order of German, Mennonite, Christian. The author went on to point out what can happen if we are not Christians first. Not just in name, but in walk also.

Just as we might seldom give thought to the groups we belong to, so it often is with the titles we carry. Though not nearly as serious as how we order our thinking, we might never have considered ourselves more than the obvious farmer, teacher, or parent. What of the more quiet titles, like cook, caregiver, or song leader? Then there are those we hope we're entitled to, like church builder or peacemaker. The list is long.

Plus, there's the list of titles we don't want to carry, and those we must avoid at all costs.

• • •

Currently, Allan and I hold quite a few obvious titles, including dad, mom, day laborer, homemaker, shop worker, and shoe store owners and keepers. We've been in the shoe business for about seven years, and we like to think we've learned some tricks of the trade. This past winter I learned some lessons I didn't learn the first time around.

Last winter, a young mother arrived at the store with her young son in tow. "I'm not sure why his boots don't fit anymore, but they don't. They look big enough for him but every time we put them on, he cries, 'Owie, owie.'"

While she was trying new boots on her tot's feet, I picked up the old pair. Strange, I mused. The boots did look big enough. Maybe the insole wasn't in properly. I reached in to check and found the culprit. There in the toe of each boot was a wadded sock!

All we got that day was a hearty laugh instead of a sale! But we've heard it said that he who laughs last, laughs loudest.

Last year's insulated boots still fit Kyle when the first snows came. Perfect. There were two pairs and no one smaller to claim them. They worked until midwinter, when he began seeing rubber boots as the footwear of choice. If we insisted he wear snow boots, he always had loud complaints of "there's something in there" or "there's something wrong with my socks." Remembering the socks-in-the-toes situation, I checked his boots carefully. I even pulled out the liners. There was nothing out of place that I could see. His socks were fine, too—maybe a little thicker for winter, but nothing exceptionally bulky.

Only after continuous complaining, during a January deep freeze, did it finally hit me. "His boots are too small!" I exclaimed to my family. Since it is never a problem to find footwear at our place—in the store, at least—we soon had a larger pair of winter boots in place. Since then, we've never heard a word about rubber boots, funny socks, or something in there.

Another important title I continue to wear, even though busy with shop work, is "baker." At least, it is to my children, and especially if it is cookies I'm baking. For them there should be cookies in the box for snacks, in lunch boxes, and with milk before bedtime (preferably with chocolate chips in them, and maybe peanut butter).

One fall, in a pamphlet filled with cookie recipes, I spied "Oatmeal Peanut Butter Cookies." They fit the criteria with their peanut butter and chocolate chips. Their simplicity won them a trial. Winners, for sure! The recipe found a permanent spot among our favorites. (The recipe is given at the end of the book.)

At our local thrift store, I found a Company's Coming cookbook devoted solely to cookies. Maybe we'll try a few more new recipes during the cold months. But when spring comes and the speed picks up, we'll go back to the tried and true.

43

After Hours

OWNING AND OPERATING a shoe store provides stories, and I like to tell them. The ones I don't enjoy as much are those the customers could, and probably do, tell on us. Maybe it's only fair that I tell some of those, too.

Most of these stories I can blame on my children. I like to take them to the store with me if possible. They enjoy unpacking boxes, and seven-year-old Alyssa is good help for showing customers where their size can be found.

While taking the children with me has its advantages, there are definitely also disadvantages. For example, consider one dark evening last fall. Supper was in the making when a customer called us out. Everyone was tired and hungry and got a tad grumpier with each customer who walked in.

Suddenly our little store was packed with after-hours customers. In an effort to keep the upper hand, I carried one boy on my hip and held the other by the hand. It was while I was writing bills that they found their little tricycle and began weaving between the customers. The shop was dark, so I couldn't send them out there. I had more than enough things to attend to that required both hands, so I decided that triking in the store would just have to pass, for once.

It didn't last. As I was totaling a bill, a loud fight erupted at the back of the store. One trike for two boys was not working tonight.

"Whee, whee," wailed loudly through the store. "Ambulance, fire truck, police coming over," one lady customer announced. "Bandages, salve, teddy bears, what do we need back here?"

The rest of the customers looked at one another, smiled, and we continued our transactions in the quiet.

More recently, we again had a customer at suppertime. This is never my favorite time of day. I'm tired and hungry and my children are too. Leaving my supper and family in their dad's capable hands, I hurried to serve our customer. At first glance, I saw that it would be easy. My customer was already finished shopping. His purchases were piled on the counter and a new pair of Sketchers was on his feet.

I wrote the receipt, adding eighty-nine dollars for the pair of safety shoes he had set beside the counter. Then, heeding Allan's advice, I checked those safety shoes for correct sizing and width. My shopper and his friends watched intently, so I explained my reason for doing this. We had prevented a lot of people from taking the wrong shoes home, I told them. It was when I turned to search for the shoebox that the polite grins turned to roars of laughter. He was quick to explain. "I, uh, actually bought those at a TSC store yesterday," he said, referring to a farm and hardware store in the area. "I just prefer to wear my new running shoes now."

I was quick to deduct eighty-nine dollars lest I gain the reputation of selling used shoes.

• • •

Since we hadn't set up a shoe booth at the annual school auction one year, I set out to enjoy the people and do some bidding. I picked the furniture tent, hoping for a bargain. All my chosen items were bringing top dollar. Hopes deflated, I was deep in conversation with my sister and a cousin when I heard twelve fifty. Now *that* was more in my range, so I spun around to see what treasure the auctioneer was selling. Two unfinished bar stools. Perfect for fitting shoes in the store, I decided as I raised my hand. Then again, and they were mine.

"Your number is?" the auctioneer asked. I reached deep into my pocket for my bidder's card, and felt a bunch of papers. Everyone was waiting, so I pulled my hand out. To my dismay, it was only a handful of the envelopes with store checks I had received earlier, Kleenex, and a burp cloth. I plunged my hand in again and pulled out more of the same.

"Marianne," my sister gasped as I deposited the stack into her hands. Around me the people were chuckling and the auctioneer was saying, "Maybe you can give the clerk your number later."

A third reach into my pocket revealed more of the same, from which a helpful bystander picked my bidder's number. Laughing helplessly, I showed it and claimed my chairs. I can't blame all my goof-ups on the children.

• • •

Part of living in Ontario means paying 13 percent harmonized sales tax (HST) for most goods and services. If you're in the business of buying and selling, every third month you must calculate the HST you collected and the HST you paid. The balance is paid to the government or a refund is requested, depending on the outcome of your calculations.

Recently, the familiar brown tax form envelope arrived, bearing the bold words NOTICE: IMPORTANT INFORMATION IN-SIDE. Alyssa claimed the sheet explaining telefiling and netfiling on the Internet. Nothing important about that information, I noted, while I happily stuck with the manual form and my familiar pen.

But the government has ways of dealing with a paper waster like me. The next quarter's brown envelope, with the important information inside, did not contain a manual form. In bold, black letters, the letter announced YOUR ELIGIBILITY TO USE CERTAIN FILING OPTIONS MAY HAVE CHANGED. I was a technology-impaired victim with two grim options. Ahead was a future filled with lengthy phone calls or paying my accountant to netfile.

The phone was my first choice, I decided, before covering the short distance to the neighborhood phone shanty. No better time than the present to see if telefiling was an option for me.

It started well enough. An automated voice greeted me before asking questions, to which I was always given a choice of two answers. All was fine until the voice requested that I enter the date of the filing period. Frantically, I scanned my papers. No filing period appeared. The voice droned on, "The numbers you have chosen are not a valid choice. If you need help, please dial the operator for assistance. Goodbye." Click.

"When you first don't succeed . . ." I muttered, carefully searching for the missing information. There it was, in its box on the top right-hand corner. Now to try, try again.

Nervously, I redialed, and then carefully pressed the correct answers to all the same questions. This time, I was ready with the filing period dates. My relief was short lived. I needed my access code. I searched unsuccessfully before the voice cut me off again. Then, there it was, just as the voice bade me farewell. I had no choice but to start the lengthy process again.

This time, I worked my way past the code question and through all the HST collectable and HST payable questions. The end was near, but the voice and I were not agreeing with the calculations. A cloud of defeat hovered near as I went for the calculator to find my mistake. Instead, I found the afternoon well worn. Baby had finished his nap and there was supper to prepare.

Automatic voices work overtime, so after supper I decided to try one more time. I dialed the now-familiar number and pushed the correct buttons for all the questions' answers. The voice repeated my selections and our calculations matched. The voice droned on, "To officially file your HST, press one for yes and zero for no." Triumphantly, I pressed 1. "Thank you. Goodbye." Click.

Weeks later, I received my HST refund check, with important information inside. By April of 2016, the government will no longer be mailing checks. Would I please fill out the direct deposit form included?

I haven't beaten them yet.

• • •

The store and our shoe and boot customers keep life spicy, though. One evening a customer interrupted my babies' bath time; both were more than happy that their father came to take over. As the minutes flew by I couldn't help but wonder what was happening in the house. I could just picture the babies still in their bathtub, looking like little wrinkled prunes. Allan thinks small clothing and little bodies are impossible, but he's a good entertainer.

My fears were calmed when I heard "Mary Had a Little Lamb" being sung loudly before I opened the door. There they all were on the glider—two little smiling heads poking out from under a fuzzy blue blanket! They were cozy, warm, and safe and sound, waiting for Mom and their pajamas.

So it goes in the Shoe Box, our community, and our home. Life is full with four children, ample family and friends, and more than enough work to keep us busy and mindful of all that we have been given. I am so grateful to God, goof-ups, modern-day frustrations, and all.

A Day in the Life of
the Author

MONDAY, JANUARY 4, 2016

5:00 a.m. The alarm beeps and I reach for the snooze button. A few minutes later always seems like a better time to get up rather than the moment. Once out of my cozy nest I open the drafts of the Pioneer Maid kitchen range and add some wood to the glowing coals. I run a wet rag and scrubber over its top to remove yesterday's cooking splatters before polishing it with furniture polish. I fill the teakettle with fresh water and set it on the hottest spot, on top of the firebox, and set the cast-iron fry pan to heat near the back of the stove. Next it's time to fill Allan's and Alyssa's lunch pails.

5:45 a.m. Allan eats his egg and toast while I have a bowl of cooked oatmeal. We drink our coffee, talk, and read from the daily devotional *Tägliches Manna* and the accompanying Scripture. Chloe Anne enjoys a quick cuddle with her dad before he leaves for his job at Horst's Welding, twenty minutes from here.

6:00 a.m. Allan's driver arrives to take him to work. Now comes the best time of day for me to pray, meditate, read, and write. If the children sleep long enough I might do some bookwork.

7:00 a.m. My early birds, Kyle and Alyssa, are up. Eric enjoys extra snooze time while I braid Alyssa's hair. I fry egg sandwiches for the children's breakfast and read them their Bible story.

8:00 a.m. Alyssa's off to school. It's too snowy to scooter so she walks the one mile to school. Chloe is tucked in her crib for her morning nap. Kyle washes the breakfast dishes and I gather laundry and head to the washroom. Fortunately, the Honda motor outside which runs my washer, roars to life with the second jerk of the starter rope. It's −18 degrees Celsius and motors can be balky in such temperatures. The motor is attached to a shaft which sets the Maytag wringer washer in motion, and before long I'm hanging laundry on my pulley washline. It soon freezes and dances crazily in the brisk wind.

9:30 a.m. Laundry and Chloe's nap are finished. I tend to the baby's needs before everyone dresses in their warm outside clothes and heads to the store. It's time to take inventory of stock for income tax purposes. I clean and rearrange boxes as I count. I haven't even finished one shelf before the boys are asking for lunch.

12:00 noon. I slide a roaster with roast beef into the oven before we eat leftovers for lunch. Eric fills the woodbox. I snatch a chapter from the book I'm reading while Chloe settles for a nap. The boys choose their storybooks. I read them aloud before we settle on the couches and recliner for our naps. I'm the only one to catch a few winks. The boys are up getting ready to go outside with Doddy and Uncle David.

1:30 p.m. I wash dishes, sweep floors, check phone messages, then mix a batch of dinner rolls, as my Guenther's Bakery bread supply is running low. No delivery until Wednesday. I add peeled whole potatoes to the roast pan. The boys are in, ready to warm up with hot chocolate and cookies. They're ready to play inside, so we'll leave the store work alone for now and I'll cut out a pair of pants for Eric instead.

3:00 p.m. I shape the dinner rolls, then work at sewing Eric's pants. I am about to sew them together when Alyssa bursts in the door, home from school. Snack time! Popping the rolls into the oven, I hurry to bring in the laundry. I am tugging at a partially frozen piece of clothing when a voice interrupts. "Hello, is the store open?" The first customer of the day at 4:00 p.m.! Owning a shoe store is unpredictable, but we're accustomed to fewer customers during January and February. We don't have the size of boots our lady customer wants, but her daughter buys a pair of gloves. I hurry back to my laundry. As I carry it to the kitchen, I think of my dinner rolls. Too late; they are dark brown. Fortunately for us, Mommy Over There had also baked bread today and sends over a beautiful loaf.

5:00 p.m. The children hang the laundry on dryers to finish drying inside. Alyssa peels carrots to cook while I make gravy and Eric sets the table. We're ready to eat our roast beef supper with canned peaches and pears for dessert when Allan walks in shortly after 5:30. Time slips by rapidly as we gather around the table to talk about our day and eat. It's Alyssa's turn to clear the table while Eric empties the lunch boxes and carries away leftovers. Allan relaxes for a few minutes with the newspaper.

7:00 p.m. Everyone's out in the shop. I'm quickly finishing dishes when another customer comes. Allan takes care of that one. We work together at the punch presses, making clips to hang up eaves troughs while the children play. Chloe enjoys wagon rides and the boys loving pulling her with the big tricycles they got for Christmas gifts.

8:00 p.m. The children hurry to ready themselves for bed so that there's more time for bedtime stories. We've just finished *Heidi* and now we're enjoying Mommy Far Away's copy of Carolyn Haywood's *Eddie's Valuable Property*.

9:00 p.m. Time to give the kitchen floor a quick sweep and then have a warm shower.

Good night and sweet dreams.

Jantzi Favorite Family Recipes

Some of these are very suitable for young cooks in the kitchen, with some supervision. Alyssa, at seven, was delighted she could find a recipe she could read.

CHOCOLATE CHIP BARS

- 1 cup butter
- 1 cup brown sugar
- 2 cups flour
- 1 cup chocolate chips

Cream butter and brown sugar. Add flour and chips. Mix well. Bake at 350°F until golden brown.

TWIX BARS

> ½ cup butter (no substitutes)
> ¾ cup brown sugar
> ½ cup white sugar
> ⅓ cup milk
> 1 cup graham cracker crumbs

Topping
1 cup chocolate chips
¾ cup peanut butter

Melt butter in a saucepan and add sugars and milk. Boil for 5 minutes. Meanwhile, spread a layer of cracker crumbs in a 9 x 13-inch pan. Pour filling evenly over crackers. Top with another layer of cracker crumbs. Cool.

To make topping, melt together chocolate chips and peanut butter. Spread over cooled squares.

CARAMEL CORN

Caramel corn should be easy enough for the children too, with some supervision with the hot syrup. Here's our recipe.

> 2 cups brown sugar
> ½ cup corn syrup
> 1 cup butter
> ½ teaspoon soda baking, mixed in a little water
> 1 teaspoon vanilla
> popcorn, popped*

Mix brown sugar, corn syrup, and butter in a saucepan. Bring to a boil for 3–5 minutes. Remove from heat and add baking soda and vanilla. Pour over popcorn. Bake at 225°F for 40–60 minutes. Once it's crispy, it's done. Be sure to stir every few minutes while it's cooling to prevent it from sticking together in a big clump.

*The original recipe calls for 8 quarts of popped corn. I like to fill two roast pans half full. Then we have a sweet treat, yet not too sweet. Suit your own tastes.

OATMEAL PEANUT BUTTER COOKIES

   1 cup sugar
   1 cup brown sugar
   1 cup shortening
   3 eggs
   1 cup peanut butter
   1½ cup flour
   1 teaspoon salt
   1 teaspoon baking soda
   1 teaspoon vanilla
   2 cups quick oats
   1 cup chocolate chips (or raisins)

Cream sugars and shortening. Add eggs and peanut butter. Beat well. Gradually add flour, salt, and baking soda. Add vanilla. Stir in quick oats and chocolate chips (or raisins). Drop by heaping teaspoonful onto a cookie sheet. Bake at 350°F for 15 minutes.

Makes 5½ dozen.

ALYSSA'S SIMPLE MUFFINS

1 egg
¼ cup vegetable oil
¾ cup milk
¼ cup sugar
1¾ cup flour
2 teaspoons baking powder

Line a muffin pan with paper liners.

Crack egg into a bowl. Beat it with a whisk. Add vegetable oil, milk, and sugar. Beat together well. Add flour and baking powder, stirring only until the flour is moistened. The batter should have small lumps. Fill liners two-thirds full of batter. Bake at 400°F for 23 minutes.

Makes 10–12 muffins.

SISTER KATHRYN'S SALSA

8 cups tomatoes, peeled and chopped
3 cups green peppers, chopped
3 cups red peppers, chopped
2 cups onions, chopped
⅓ cup hot peppers, chopped
1½ cup white vinegar
2 tablespoons salt
2 tablespoons sugar
2 tablespoons parsley
2 teaspoons paprika
2 teaspoons oregano
1½ cup tomato paste

Combine everything except the tomato paste and cook, uncovered, for 1 hour. Stir in tomato paste and simmer 10 minutes. Jar and seal.

FAQs about the Amish: The Author Answers

Author Marianne Jantzi answers some frequently asked questions about Amish life, faith, and culture.

1. What are some of the things Old Order Amish do for social life in your community?

Weddings are big social and religious occasions. Each summer we have about seven to ten weddings in our community of approximately 236 households. With a total of 1,107 people, 146 of these are young folk. We travel by van to attend weddings in our three "daughter" communities, which are too far to reach easily by horse and buggy.

Some in our community enjoy horse auctions and sales. Our neighbors are in charge of the annual spring and fall Great Canadian Dutch Harness Horse Sale. Monthly horse sales also draw large crowds.

Hunting, fishing, and quiltings are activities we look forward to.

2. How many schools do you have and what are they like?

There are ten church districts and eight schools. The majority of these schools are one room with two teachers and about thirty students total. On the last or second-to-last day of school, each will host an annual school picnic. The morning is spent competing in races, high jumps, ball throws, and group games. A highlight is always the tug-of-war. After lunch everyone joins in or watches the ball game.

3. Are the customs you describe here for wedding, church services, and funerals the same from one Amish community to the next?

Although there will always be similarities, the small details will vary between communities. For instance, at our wedding services as I describe in this book, a small amount of wine is generally served at the meal after the wedding. Other Amish communities do not do that.

4. Does the girl on the cover reflect the dress style of your community?

Doesn't she look happy? Just like my oldest daughter does when she has paper and pen in hand. But no, the cover girl's clothing and covering style are unique to the community she belongs to, just as we dress according to the standards of our community.

The Author

MARIANNE JANTZI is an Amish writer and homemaker. Formerly a teacher in an Amish school, Jantzi now educates and inspires through her Northern Reflections column for the *Connection*, a magazine directed mainly to Amish and plain communities across North America. She and her husband have four young children and run a shoe store in the Milverton Amish community of Ontario, Canada.